JUST BREATHE

How Yoga Can Release Stress and Tension

Amanda Gabrielle

10-10-10
Publishing

Just Breathe - How Yoga Can Release Stress and Tension
www.thebreatheandrelaxbook.com

ISBN: 978-1-77277-397-2

Published by:
10-10-10 Publishing
Markham, Ontario

First 10-10-10 Publishing paperback edition November 2020

Contents

Dedication vii
Foreword ix
Acknowledgments xi

Chapter One: Stress Less with Yoga 1
Happiness Is Basic to Human Nature 1
What You Need to Know about Stress 2
The Price We Pay 3
Take a Breath and Slow Down 5
Yoga's Formula for Stressing Less 7

Chapter Two: How Yoga Can Help 15
The "Branches" of Yoga 15
What All Branches of Yoga Have in Common 20
Finding Your Path 20
My Story 21
What Yoga Is Not 24
How Yoga Can Help 26

Chapter Three: Learn How to "Deep Breathe" Your Stress Away .. 33
The Importance of Oxygen and How the Lungs Work 33
Alleviate Stress Through the Simple Practice of Yogic Breathing 35
Yogic Breathing Techniques 36
Breathing Your Way into Postures 43

Chapter Four: Warm Up Before Stretching 47
Why Warm Up? 47
What Is Fascia, and Why Is It Important to Warm Up? 48
How to Improve Fascia Health 49
Awaken the Feet..50
Respect the Body's Need to Warm Up 51
How to Begin Your Yoga Practice 52
Seven Warm-up Exercises 54

Chapter Five: Eight Beginner-Friendly Yoga Poses 61
That Awaken Your Inner Wisdom
The Essence of a Pose 61
Some Tips Before Beginning Your Yoga Practice 63
The Asanas 64

Chapter Six: Use It or Lose It 81
The Importance of a Daily Practice 81
The Advantages of Doing Yoga 82
How to Practice 83
Creating Posture Sequences...85
Sample of a Posture Sequence 87

Chapter Seven: Time to Relax 93
The Relaxation Response...94
Benefits of "Letting Go" and Deep Relaxation...............................95
Tips for a Successful Relaxation Practice 97
Relaxation Techniques..98
Making Time to Relax..104

Chapter Eight: Time to Meditate 107
What Meditation Is 108
Benefits of Meditating 109
Tips on Starting Your Own Meditation Practice...........................110
Ways to Meditate 111
Guided Seated Meditation 113
How Do You Know If It Is Working? 114

Chapter Nine: Seven Ways to Be More Mindful and 117
Happier Every Day!
Yoga and Mindfulness – The Connection 118
What Is Mindful Yoga? 119
The Benefits of Yoga and Mindfulness 121
How to Find Moments to Be Mindful Throughout Your Day.........122

Epilogue..127
About the Author 135

This book is dedicated to my daughters, Olivia and XiaoRan, who inspire me and fill my life with love and light. You both continue to amaze me with joy. I am so grateful we have been brought together as a family, and for being shown that I am truly blessed.

Foreword

Are you feeling anxiety and confusion, especially during these troubled, unprecedented times? Would you like to feel fully present and alive with every breath, filling each moment with peace and joy?

In this user-friendly book, author Amanda Gabrielle introduces you to the fundamentals of yoga breathing and poses and shows you how to incorporate them into your daily routine. She enlightens you as to the mindful and spiritual benefits that yoga offers.

For the past three decades, Amanda has taught yoga to hundreds of people and now is sharing with you what she has found gainful and enriching in her own life. This book will transform your way of coping with stress and tension.

Whether you are in your teens or your "golden age," new to yoga or a seasoned practitioner, you can use the tools within *Just Breathe* to develop your own strategy to cope with these challenging times. This book is an essential addition to your survival kit in life.

Take a journey by reading this fascinating book and develop your own unique strategies to live a healthy, happy and fulfilled life.

Raymond Aaron
New York Times Bestselling Author

Acknowledgments

First and foremost, I am deeply grateful to **Raymond Aaron,** my publisher. You have transformed this idea I had of writing a book, into a book, and have brought it out into the world! Secondly, I express my gratitude to the **10-10-10 program** team, especially **Liz** and **Wasque,** whose assistance and guidance brought this project to the finish line. Also, the editors and those formatting in the program have been invaluable. A special thank you to the illustrators of this book, **Olivia** and **XiaoRan**, who always make my journey on this planet easier, kinder, and full of surprises (good ones).

My yoga teachers, who have inspired and awed me with their knowledge and wisdom, |I wish to extend my love and gratitude; I am indebted to each of you. Whether my time was brief with you or over a number of years, your spirit comes through me. I want to thank the following people: **Ellen McLean**, our journey began over 30 years ago, when you invited me to your yoga class; you are kindness and generosity. **Nitya Kandath**, my guru and friend in India, you are one who "walks the talk." Your knowledge and dedication to teaching yoga is superlative (and thank you for always welcoming us into your home). **Nan Gumley**, my yoga certification instructor at **Sheridan College** in Oakville, you made yoga genuine and acceptable as a recognized credit course at an Ontario institute. **Lilias Folan**, "the first lady of yoga," I am thankful for the times (Niagara Falls retreat and

Kripalu Center) that I have learned the humbleness of yoga from you. **Ken (Nateshva) Scott,** you are an amazing, creative visionary who made yoga come alive with dance. I admire how you were able to encourage us to express ourselves with ease and confidence. Through **Contact Yoga,** you showed us how to be open-minded and to live in the present moment. **Erin Maile O'Keefe** and **Kevin O'Keefe**, founders of **Circus Yoga**, my daughters and I have enjoyed attending your workshops over the past 15 years. They have been a truly a transformational experience. I didn't think it was possible to have so much fun while practicing yoga. You inspired us to conquer our fears and be more open-minded. **Yoga Centre Toronto (Marlene)** and **London (Karen and Sue)**, I remember those early morning classes that kept me aligned—thank you!

Of course, I wish to send a thank you out to all my friends for being such amazing people and for believing in me. You inspire me every day; you have been my "life support" team and have kept me going in terms of physical and mental health. Thanks to: **Martha, Anna, and Minhly**, Richmond Hill P and P; **Donna E, Maida I, Paula B, Danielle, and Lida** (Massage Perfect); and my "fav" boss, **Greg D.,** London P and P; and **Neena** and the gang. **Elaine D.**, I am especially thankful for your encouragement and helpful feedback. I am deeply appreciative to **Deb W.** (Ottawa); you encourage me to take risks and learn new things and be the best person I can be. My friends are truly remarkable people, and I am so lucky to have every one of you in my life!

I extend my gratitude to the following wonderful people, who have contributed to this book by either giving me opportunities to grow and learn through teaching, or by offering great, practical life advice: **Barb Armstrong**, CSEP, fitness supervisor, town of Stouffville, thank you for giving me the opportunity to share with so many adults and families all the benefits that yoga has to offer, and for your ongoing support of me in all my yoga endeavors. **Sue Gerrard**, physiotherapist, Joint Venture, thank you for giving me a space to teach when I was first starting out in Stouffville. **Pamela Holt,** owner of Holt School of Reflexology, I admire your knowledge and dedication in the field of reflexology. Your willingness to share your wisdom with me and others has added greatly to my "tools" for better health and happier living. **Jennifer Holt**, Holt Counselling, London, you are a superb counselor! Thank you for reminding me to take the time to stop, listen, and breathe, and to find my inner wisdom. **Tabith Liston**, Health and Wellness manager, Bostwick YMCA, London, thank you for your open-mindedness and for giving XiaoRan and myself the opportunity to share our love of circus yoga with the families in this community center.

Edward Pugliese, career counselor at LEHC, and my career guru, thank you for the support and encouragement in continuing to pursue my lifelong passions, including the writing of this book. **Lorry Pasternak**, CPA, thank you for the many years of ensuring that I always stayed on track financially with the Government of Canada. **Judy Fleming**, director of H. Acres Canada, you are such a remarkable person, whose dedication and knowledge of health and nutrition changed my life. I will be forever grateful and miss you very much. **Alma Botcharova**, fellow author, thank you for your encouragement! (I can't wait to read your book!)

The following organizations have influenced me in realizing the value of helping others, and/or helped me in achieving my own successes:

The Psychology Foundation of Canada: I would like to acknowledge the amazing work they do with children and stress. I enjoyed and gained great satisfaction from being a program accredited facilitator in the past, and I continue to follow their work with the **Kids Have Stress** program.

Thanks to **Claire** and **Shawn (V.O.N.),** I have learned so much by teaching the seniors' classes at Richmond Wood and Masonville Manor and Lucan. They are such amazing people, and they are an inspiration and a testimony that "aging" does not have to mean feeling old.

West Alliance Church (WLA) Community Garden group: What a wonderful way to celebrate community. My involvement with you has brought such joy and satisfaction. It is so true that your mind, body, and overall well-being can all benefit from getting your hands dirty (gardening).

CNIB – Ryan V, program lead, and **Terri-Lyn**, yoga student: Volunteering to teach yoga to people with vision impairments has made me a better teacher and person. The participants have taught me a lesson in resilience, and, with each class, I continue to be inspired by their willingness and courage to try something new. I hope to keep teaching these classes for many years!

To my family, who uplifts me, I wish to acknowledge:

Clarkes of London: My parents, **Bernice and Tom**, brothers **Ken** and **Guy**, and **Gail "GG" Clarke** (Thanks for the introduction to the **Probus Club of South London** the friendliest people I have ever met!); nieces and nephew, **Claireese, Chris, Jake, and Kieren**; **Maria** (Thanks for the tech support.); **Sheila** (Thanks for the massages.); and **Kaley**. Clarkes of Smith Falls and Woodstock Saving the best for last, I am unable to express in mere words how much love, joy, and adventure that my darling daughters, **Olivia and XiaoRan,** have created for me. I am truly blessed that you are both in my life!

To my awesome yoga students, I am so grateful!! A special acknowledgment to the students from **Stouffville United Church**: **Cindy and Frank, Jane and Anna, Nancy F., Andy and Nancy C., Rita, Barb T., Danielle, Pat, Carol F., Ann P.,** and the many others who joined us throughout the years. I could not have done this book without our years together. Your trust in me, your willingness to try every new approach to yoga, and your generous and open hearts were a constant inspiration. I appreciated your questions, stories (families), and commitment to yoga, and most of all, the love and laughs we shared. You made teaching so enjoyable! To all my students, each of you have been an education for me. You have taught me lessons I never thought I needed to learn. You are my great teachers!! Thank you; I carry your divine light carefully and gratefully in my heart!! Namaste!! Amanda

Chapter One

Stress Less with Yoga

"In our natural state, we are glorious beings."
– Marianne Williamson

Happiness Is Basic to Human Nature

Happiness is a basic goal of our human nature. However, it is easily forgotten in our hectic lifestyles. Stress undermines our health and well-being. To realize this innate goal, we must deal constructively with stressors that we are met with in everyday life. No one is exempt from this reality. Luckily, yoga can help! We were not created to live worried, bitter, upset, tense, or stressed lives. It is a fundamental desire of every human being to live in a state of happiness, health, and fulfillment. Our natural state is to live as "glorious beings."

We must establish a positive outlook in life, with a strategy—a strategy for being optimistic in life, with the development of contentment that allows us to make the best of any situation. It is important that when bad things happen, you deal with them in a positive and balanced way. Yoga is especially suited to gain control over stress responses.

Yoga is a tradition of skillful, conscious living that has been around for thousands of years and has held its value over time. It is as valuable today as it was in ancient times. For me, the joy of yoga initially was in the form of its physical helpfulness, but it also led the way to enhancing my emotional hardiness and mental well-being. I have found that my yoga students are looking for emotional and spiritual connection as well as the physical aspects. But they are also seeking ways to manage their day-to-day stresses.

What You Need to Know about Stress

Stress has existed as long as humans have, for it is part of our machinery. It gives valuable signals to us as to the choices we make and the directions we take. Some stress is normal and can help us. But people don't realize what is building up in their bodies and minds with too much stress, whether it is from lack of sleep, stress on the job, or trying to live up to some illusions. There are more people living unhappy lives than I would care to compute. Since 9/11, people have been fearful. They feel insecure and unsteady about the world's situation. The present-day coronavirus (COVID-19) has left us feeling vulnerable. People have been isolated, feeling anxious, and depressed. This makes people negative. It is easy to go around worried about our future and all the difficulties over which we have little or no control. It is easy to get stressed over finances or frustrated with loved ones. We are tempted to feel guilty about our past mistakes and be bitter about what did not work out. And then we wonder why we don't enjoy our lives, why we are not passionate about our dreams, and why we can't sleep at night. It is because there are so many problems created by life itself, and it is so overwhelming and stressful that we have difficulty finding the joy and happiness we all deserve.

The Price We Pay

Stress has many causes, and world fear makes people tentative and insecure. We devote ourselves to jobs that allow us no time off. We spend hours a day commuting. People struggle financially. We are bombarded with images of perfection, especially with our youth. They must be too thin and too perfect!

There is this constant encouragement to be competitive (at such young ages) and always striving to be better than the next one. Even as we get older, there is the illusion of remaining young. Major life changes, such as divorce, death in the family, moving, or retirement, are some things in life that we cannot avoid. And we can't avoid change such as technology. But with change comes consequences, some positive and some not. For example, I have seen people indiscriminately enraptured with technology, much the way that we can be with food. Our diets—the very foods that shape and fuel our bodies—have shifted more toward processed foods, a phenomenon from which we are only now starting to recognize the drawbacks. Social media, a huge component of technological change, is quite like the shift toward processed food. In that, we are drawn away from a genuine experience that holds the value of life experiences and replaces it with only a "processed" virtual experience that cannot provide the same tactile and developmental experience as an authentic interaction. Unless you make the world stop in its tracks and behave the way you think it should, we need to find a way to carve out an oasis and find the peace in us and around us.

Some stress is expected and can help us. But people don't realize, with too much stress, what is building up in their bodies. Back in the caveman days, when you would meet a woolly mammoth, you would fight it or flee the situation. It is our sympathetic nervous systems that deal with the fight or flight response. It is a very primitive reflex in the body that deals with stressful situations. With continuous stress, what happens in our bodies is that we get stuck in this "revved-up" situation, and it becomes so familiar to us that we likely do not consciously realize what is happening to us.

The price of stress we experience is phenomenal. It can be tension in the neck and shoulders, or in the lower back; it can be chronic headaches, indigestion, the inability to sleep, heart disease, etc. There are so many ways in which the body reacts to stress on a day-to-day basis. The list goes on and on. Being irritable, moody, and having memory problems, having difficulty thinking and concentrating, having so many things on your to-do list that there would not be enough hours in the day to complete, and you literally cannot focus and are constantly worrying and feeling so overwhelmed that you have difficulty making decisions, are all signs of stress. Stress is so harmful to our mental health. Feeling helpless and hopeless is devastating. Being anxious, unhappy, and depressed are signs of extreme stress.

Take a Breath and Slow Down

The flip side of this fight or flight response is found in the parasympathetic nervous system and what is called the rest and relaxation response, which immediately sounds much better! What happens is that the parasympathetic system calms us down. It is that loss of the rest and relaxation response that this book addresses, and how by using the breath and yoga can bring balance into your life and reboot this rest and relaxation response. Today we live our lives in fast forward, and I want us to live our lives in slow motion and be present so that we are slowing everything down. If I could do one thing as a yoga teacher, I would try to convince my students to TAKE A BREATH AND SLOW DOWN and be present in what they are doing. I think the term that is commonly used today is "mindful."

One of the things you might find as you read this book and try some of the practices, is that because your nervous system is so revved up, slowing down might initially make you irritable. Your first experience may bother you. As one of my students once told me, it is like running and suddenly hitting a brick wall. It took the student a long time to realize that you must slow down to stop. I have found that those who often resist yoga are those that need it the most. Another common reaction during the beginning of a yoga practice is crying. It is the "letting go" for the first time in a long time. To be able to slow down and stop allows you the opportunity to tune into the sensitivity and the natural "inner wisdom" you have inside you.

The techniques described in this book are designed for you, with the understanding that you have the power within yourself to help you release tension and stress. This is the beauty of yoga.

At its core, yoga is a solitary practice, and at its heart as well. It is just yoga, your body, and your breath, in the quietness of your space. Yoga allows you to re-acquaint yourself with the peaceful, content, perfect part of you.

Hatha yoga (which I teach) is one "branch" of a much larger practice of yoga (more on the branches of yoga in the next chapter). The essence of the teaching is that we are all perfect at our core. We are all glorious beings. I had a yoga teacher say that yoga is the "unlearning" of what we have learned about ourselves throughout our lives. Our parents tell us who we are; our schools, churches, and friends all tell us who we are—with good intentions or not. This sometimes leads us to believe certain things about ourselves that are not true. The patterns or beliefs that we have developed are like clouds surrounding us, blocking the sun; the sun being our true "self," our perfect glorious being, free from extreme stress and physical and mental harm. When we practice yoga, it is like having the sun inside, brightening and then burning away the cloud. Often, you will see people in a yoga class meet each other with the greeting "Namaste," which means, "I acknowledge the 'light' in you," or the "Divine" within you.

Yoga is a vital part of releasing this power we have in all of us, to realize our true selves. It helps us to "tap" into the forces and to utilize strengths within us that are not otherwise readily available or known to us.

Yoga's Formula for Stressing Less

Yoga acknowledges that there must be harmony between the body, mind, and spirit to live a healthy, happy, fulfilling life. The formula for living a less stressed, amazing life is in the congruity between these elements. To achieve this rapport, yoga offers you the necessary "tools." The tools available through yoga are the yoga poses, specific breathing techniques, relaxation and meditation practices, and mindfulness. It is the breath that connects body, mind, and spirit. Through the tools in yoga, one can discover their strengths, insights, power, and what is needed to have balance and control in their own lives. These newfound discoveries and heightened awareness pave the path that leads you to self, the core of your being.

Within this book, I present you with the tools that yoga has to offer, which allow for not just a wonderful and comprehensive yoga practice in its own right, but shows you how these tools can be applied in your own day-to-day stresses. The chapters give you the opportunity to pick and choose techniques to create your own strategies for releasing stress and tension in your life. Breathing techniques to combat stress are explained. There is a chapter on rest and relaxation, which is so, so important for coping with stress. There are several yoga poses you can choose from, as well as a sample sequence to ensure that every part of your body releases and lets go of any tension. The chapters incorporate how the body, mind, and spirit are bridged together by the breath.

I have trained and taught yoga for over 30 years. My classes always include breathing and relaxation exercises, which are some of the tools that can be used to combat stressful times. This book follows a sequence of what would be a typical class of mine. You will notice that there is rhythm to the sequence— an ebb and flow, breathing in and breathing out. This is repeated in all classes. This concept of rhythm and repetition, when brought into everyday life, is very beneficial.

It was brought to my attention many years ago when my daughters were attending a Waldorf school in Toronto, Canada. Rudolf Steiner, founder of the educational philosophy of Waldorf education, referred to the need to give children a daily rhythmical flow of activities that allowed for the child to breathe with natural ease—to live as we breathe, an ebb and flow of breathing in and breathing out. This rhythm and repetition allows for the security of knowing and trusting, as it relieves the burden of wondering what is going to happen next. It allows the opportunity to be present in the moment, which is being mindful. The many benefits of being mindful are given in the last chapter of this book.

Yoga changes your self-awareness. I have found it easiest to initially work with and concentrate on the physical realm to bring change. This seems to be a natural starting point for most people, perhaps because of the tangibility of the improvements that result. The gains in the physical realm then lay a foundation for strengthening and developing the other realms of our being (i.e. mind, spirit, and self),   which will then allow us to be better equipped and prepared to approach difficult, stressful situations in our lives. One example of how yoga's effect on self-awareness has been put into my practice during my teachings relates to the flexibility of the spine and the flexibility of the mind. When teaching, I ensure that the spine moves in all directions with the postures. I have come to believe that you are as young as your spine is flexible. A stiff body may be an indicator of an inflexible mind, which may be an obstacle in coping skills. While the postures of yoga work on your "outward being," meditation and relaxation help you to release inwardly. It is remarkable how yoga and relaxation restore the harmonious function of the body and mind. Yoga seeks to relax your body, which is the temple of the soul.

Moving forward in the book, we will examine what I have called the Yoga 360 Degree Intervention model. It is an overview approach that can be used to remind us of the principles we are attempting to put into practice, and help sustain continued growth .The model can be used as another "tool" that recognizes the necessity for harmony between the body, mind, and spirit, if we are going to live healthy, happy, and fulfilled lives. You can't be physically healthy until you are mentally and emotionally healthy. Finding the balance between these elements leads us to our authentic, wise, true selves. The chapters of this book incorporate the Yoga 360 model, and how the body, mind, and spirit are bridged together through the breath. There is a model diagram at the end of this chapter to help visualize those areas in your life. As we move along, using the tools of yoga, and the insights and awareness discovered, you will be able to identify areas where you may need balance, as well as where your strengths are.

The desire to release stress, and the ability to do so, is a process. Just as you strengthen muscles, you can strengthen and re-pattern your nervous system. It is very similar to the way you increase muscle strength. When you start, you may find it difficult to keep focus. You may be agitated because you're not getting the results fast enough. Far too often, for example, I see beginners trying so hard to relax, which of course results in the opposite of what one must do to relax. There is a wonderful Buddhist saying that the difficult thing about relaxing and meditation (and of course, yoga is preparation for meditation) is the doing of nothing. The ability to do less and do nothing at all is a skill worth developing, so my point is: Be PATIENT and MAKE TIME! Discover what strengths, insights, and awareness reveal themselves when you SLOW DOWN and do NOTHING.

If you only have 15 minutes to do your practice, don't stress; just do something even for a few deep breaths. I can always tell the folks who make a resolution to practice every day for an hour or more. A word of caution: Don't bite off more than you can chew; start small. It will draw you in, and your body and sense of well-being will motivate you. You will find that 15 minutes becomes 30 minutes without having realized it, and the next thing you know, you have practiced for an hour. You will find that more benefit comes from 15–20 minutes, a few times a week, than trying to do and learn everything once a month.

I have been practicing yoga for many years and have realized the beauty of yoga and the depth of yoga. Every passing year continues to change me. My practice has evolved. While in the beginning I felt myself become more physically strong, and my flexibility increased, the most radical change has been on the spiritual and emotional level. As my focus changed, I could see that the best part for me was the change in my nervous system. This change has allowed the relaxation/rest response to be repatterned into my body, and I have realized that the breath is everything. The breath has really found its place in my practice. My physical practice changed enormously; it is more comfortable, and I can hold poses much longer—everything feels better when I use my breath. I can focus outside the physical body and deal with a stressful situation in a more emotionally and spiritually balanced way.

We can't stop negative things from happening, but we can keep them from staying. The past is over; this is a new day. One of the most important things we can do for ourselves to promote contentment is to cut ourselves some slack. I find it is a misconception to think that everyone else has their act together—they don't! You are not the only one struggling to cope in this stressful world that we live in. We are all in the same boat, which I think can be a source of reassurance where we can give each other support.

Happiness and peace are achievable, and the process for obtaining is not complicated. Rather than emphasizing the manner in which people manifest stress, let us proceed to the formula and tools that yoga can offer, as laid out in this book, for putting misery-producing stress in its place, and start living in our natural state of good health, happiness, and fulfillment as the glorious beings we are!

In this book, I gather my best ideas and knowledge of yoga to help you stretch, breathe, and meditate your way through the challenging times. Whether you need to get rest, get moving, get "grounded," or just get a grip on your life and learn to slow down, this book is loaded with real tools to help you regain your balance and strength in the face of any grueling obstacles. Whatever your reason for picking up this book, I think you will find a gentle but powerful approach to help you understand how your breath and yoga can naturally become an integral aspect of your life, and help manage your stress. The next chapter reveals much more detail on exactly *how yoga can help you!!* READ ON! Each chapter builds on the previous one.

Yoga 360° Intervention Model

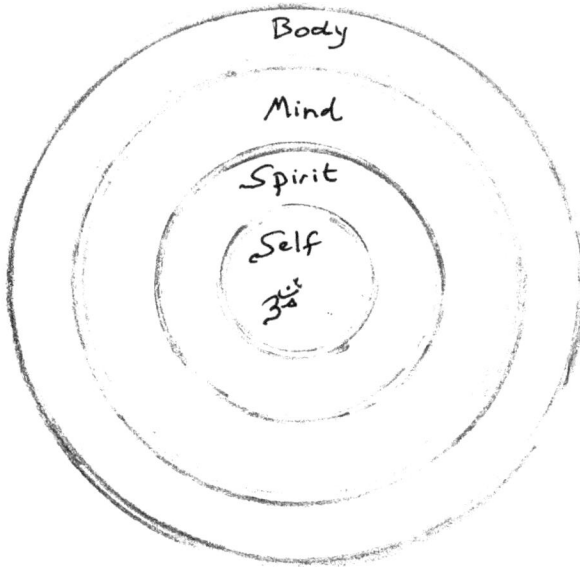

Yoga acknowledges there must be harmony between the body, mind, and spirit to live your best life. Finding balance between these elements leads us to our authentic wise true self.

ॐ – This is the yoga symbol for the word/sound "OM." Symbols in yoga can be used as highly effective tools for calming the mind and unleashing immense potential within oneself.

To explore the intriguing meaning behind some of yoga's most popular symbols, go to www.thebreatheandrelaxbook.com.

Notes

_____

_____

_____

_____

_____

_____

_____

_____

_____

_____

_____

_____

_____

Chapter Two

How Yoga Can Help

"Health is wealth, peace of mind is happiness,
yoga shows the way."
— Vishnudevanada Saraswati

The "Branches" of Yoga

Although yoga appears everywhere, with classes being held at recreation departments (I taught for many years with the Markham and Stouffville Parks Departments), health clubs, physiotherapy offices (I also taught at Joint Venture Physio clinic in Stouffville), in church basements (thanks to Stouffville United Church for many years of collaboration), and at numerous yoga centers, yoga does not have its roots in the North American fitness industry.

It is believed that yoga has been around for over 5,000 years and originated in India. The word *yoga* comes from the ancient *Sanskrit language* spoken by the traditional elite of India, the Brahmins. *Yoga* means "to join" or "union." Yoga seeks unity at various levels: physical, mental, and spiritual. In ancient times, yoga was often compared to a tree with roots and branches.

Within the philosophy of yoga, there are six distinct "branches" of yoga: Raja, Bhakti, Karma, Jnana, Tantra, and Hatha. Each branch of yoga has its unique characteristics and functions and represents a particular approach to life. However, all branches of yoga seek to achieve the same final goal of *enlightenment.* In yoga, it is a state of "awakened" understanding. To be enlightened is to be freed from the control of the mind and to experience deep spiritual peace.

In this following section, I will give you a brief description of these six branches of yoga.

Raja Yoga

Raja means "royal." It is also known as *classical yoga*, and meditation is the focal point of this branch of yoga. This distinguished approach involves strict adherence to the eight "limbs" of yoga as outlined by *Patanjali* in the *Yoga Sutras*. Patanjali was an Indian sage who is believed to have authored the *Yoga Sutras*, which are designed to lead to enlightenment. They follow in this order:

- *Yama* – refers to moral self-discipline, consisting of the practices of non-violence, truthfulness, chastity, non-stealing, and non-attachment.

- *Niyama* – self-restraint, involving self-study, unpretentious-ness, and devotion to a higher principle

- *Asana* – yoga postures (This limb type of yoga is what most of us are familiar with in the Western world.)

- *Pranayama* – involves breath control, which influences your physical health and mental concentration

- Pratayahara – involves the withdrawal of senses, meaning the outer world is not a distraction from our inner selves

- *Dharana* – concentration, or your ability to prolong focusing, which is essential for yogic meditation

- *Dhyana* – meditation, the practice of higher yoga

- *Samadhi* – ecstasy or final liberation. In yoga, this is the final stage and highest at which one experiences oneness with the universe.

Note: Please do not be intimidated by all the unfamiliar words. Along the way, I will be introducing you to Sanskrit terms and their meanings.

Raja yoga attracts those individuals who are introspective and drawn to meditation. For example, members of religious orders and spiritual communities devote themselves to this branch of yoga.

Karma Yoga

The principle of Karma yoga is that what we experience today is created by our actions of the past. If we act unselfishly, without attachment and with integrity, we are creating a future free of negativity, and are influencing our future positively. This path of yoga is also known as the path of service. We practice Karma yoga through our work and how we live our lives. Serving others, such as volunteering for a non-profit organization, is an example of selfless service associated with the Karma yoga path.

Bhakti Yoga

Bhakti yoga is the path of devotion and seeing the Divine in all creations. This path of yoga provides an opportunity to cultivate acceptance and tolerance for everyone. Followers of this path express their devotional nature in their every thought, word, and action, whether they are doing the dishes or calming the anger of a loved one.

Jnana Yoga

Jnana yoga is the path of the sage or scholar. It is the yoga of the mind and requires development of the intellect through the study of the scriptures and the texts of the yogic tradition. Because it involves serious study, it appeals to those who are intellectually inclined. Within the context of Western traditions, Jesuit priests and Benedictine monks, as well as Kabbalistic scholars, are examples of Jnana yogis.

Tantra Yoga

This branch of yoga is the most complex and misunderstood of all the yogic branches. Tantra is the pathway of the ritual in which one experiences the Divine in everything they do. In the Western world, and in India, Tantra yoga has become associated with sexual rituals. Although sexual rituals are used in some schools of Tantra yoga, most actually recommend a celibate lifestyle. The purpose of Tantra yoga is to cultivate a reverential approach to life in order to further one's emotional well-being.

This type of yoga would appeal to those who enjoy ceremonies. Those who practice this path of yoga would appreciate all types of ceremonies, including a Japanese tea ceremony or the consecration of the Eucharist in a Catholic mass.

Another name for Tantra yoga is *Kundalini yoga*. The name means "she who is coiled," and suggests that there is a secret "serpent power" that Tantra yoga can cultivate. This is latent spiritual energy stored in the body.

Hatha Yoga

It is the physical aspect of yoga, and the focus of much of this book. Hatha yoga was developed as a vehicle for meditation. Hatha yoga practitioners believe that unless the body is properly purified and prepared, the higher stages of meditation and ecstasy are impossible to achieve. It is the most practical of the yogas as it addresses the body, breath, and mind, and requires discipline and effort, as do the other branches of yoga.

Hatha yoga is the style of yoga I teach, which incorporates the body, the breath, and the mind. At the end of this chapter, you will find a depiction of "The Yoga Tree and the Six Branches of Yoga."

What All Branches of Yoga Have in Common

All branches of yoga share at least three fundamental practices: *conscious breathing*, *awareness*, and *relaxation*.

- *Conscious* B*reathing* – I was taught that the breath is the bridge between the body and mind. In yoga, the breath is used to cultivate awareness and relaxation.

- *Awareness* – In yoga, this means to be consciously present, aware of sensations in your body, and aware of your thoughts, but being aware as an observer or as a "witness," only in a non-judgmental and non-attached way. This is what being mindful would be.

- *Relaxation* – This is the conscious release of unnecessary tension; and therefore, the release of unhealthy tension in the body.

Both awareness and relaxation are fundamental to a yoga practice, because without the conscious awareness and the ability to release tension through relaxation, any exercise would be just exercise, not yogic exercise.

Finding Your Path

You may already be involved in one or more of these branches of yoga. For example, you may already be a Hatha *yogi* or *yogini,* practicing the postures with a teacher or by yourself. Just to clarify, someone who is dedicated to the discipline of balancing the body and mind through yoga, is traditionally called a yogi (if male) or yogini (if female). I use both terms randomly throughout this book or refer to one as a yoga practitioner.

If you are volunteering at a hospice or participating at a local food bank, you are actively practicing Karma yoga. Perhaps reading this book sparked an interest in the study of yoga philosophy—or in my case, a trip to India, which set me on the path of Jnana yoga.

You need to know that you are not limited to one path. You may practice Hatha yoga, taking care of your physical body, while at the same time practicing a lifestyle of a Bhakti yogi, expressing compassion for everything in life.

You must trust that whichever avenue of yogic expression draws your interest, it will probably be the right path for you. The more I practiced and got to know myself better, the path became clearer.

My Story

You may have seen pictures of yoga contortionists, with their limbs tied in knots, or heard about "power yoga" or "hot yoga" classes. They may have persuaded you that yoga is not something you could possibly do. If so, I hope to show you that there is so much more to yoga, and that virtually anyone can do it! This includes those who start out with very little strength, energy, or flexibility. And whether you are aged 15, 30, 60, or beyond, and new to yoga, I will guide you to your own individual expression of physical and emotional freedom through yoga.

While yoga has been a part of much of my life, it was not always. I was always very athletic, playing many sports, including baseball, basketball, swimming, etc. But I was not one who could readily bend my body into a pretzel (and still can't). I came to yoga in my late 20s and found it challenging. But in this challenge, I've seen a steady growth in what I can do and how good I feel—not just physically but in my mental state, especially in dealing with stress. The more I put into my practice, the greater the rewards have become. Like many people who play sports, I never did pay much attention to stretching. I started out incredibly stiff. I had difficulty with even the most basic poses; with straight legs, I couldn't touch the floor with my fingers. I had difficulty straightening my spine, let alone bending it backwards.

I was drawn to yoga and began attending classes after moving to Toronto, Canada, from a much smaller town, and while starting a highly demanding career. The move to a "big" city, and beginning work as a probation/parole officer, was very stressful for me. I quickly came to enjoy the feeling of peace that the yoga classes gave to me. I began inserting yoga into the "cracks" in my days, even if my schedule was crazy and I could only fit in a few minutes a day. If I was sitting at my computer or had a break between appointments, I'd take a minute to stretch my arms over my head to release tension in my shoulders. Or I would bend forward, place my hands on my desk, and lengthen my spine for a few seconds. Have you ever watched a cat or a dog as they lengthen their spines with all kinds of stretches? In yoga, we say that you are as young as your spine is flexible. *As you stretch, you relax, and you release stress and tension* in the body and mind!

I spent many hours driving on my commute to work each day. Yoga taught me to pay more attention to my body, noticing the way my shoulders tended to slump as I sat behind the steering wheel. My massage therapist at work, Lida, would remind me to sit up tall—thank you! I began to practice yoga regularly, and amazing things started to happen. After only a few months, my chronic slouching improved. I stood taller. My flexibility and strength increased. I continued to play sports, without injury, and learned how to stretch properly.

I enrolled in yoga teacher training at Sheridan College, in Oakville, Ontario, and became a Certified Yoga Instructor in 1987. I continued with many courses and training over the next 25 years. I have been attending seminars and training at yoga centers in both Canada and the United States, as well as taking trips to India. Most recently, in 2018, I was able to travel to India with my two daughters, where we lived with my yoga teacher and his family, in the Province of Kerala, India. I was first there in 1997, with Nitya Kandath, who is the founder and master teacher of Nitya Sudhana Kudir Ashram, in Kerala, South India. It is a beautiful yoga retreat center. He continues to offer teachers teachings and other workshops. I can personally recommend Nitya, and he can be reached via his website at www.nityayoga.com. I have always continued to educate myself on many aspects of yoga, including teaching children and working with special needs groups. Most recently, I have connected with the Canadian National Institute for the Blind, to begin teaching yoga to the blind. I also have a special interest in how yoga can help kids, because kids have stress too! It is so enjoyable for me to teach such diverse groups, and I take whatever opportunities I can to share my knowledge and experience of yoga.

Perhaps even more profound than yoga's physical effect on me were the mental and emotional benefits. Once I developed a regular practice, I noticed a change in my outlook on life. Problems didn't seem to get to me as much. I did not seem to worry as much. Without even consciously trying, more and more, I seemed to be doing what yoga philosophy teaches: Be present in what you are doing, be sincere in your effort, and without judging or being attached to the end result. Being the observer or the witness only "frees" you. What has become more important to me is the mental peace that has come, the sense of gratitude and reverence, and the gradual but sometimes sudden opening of some previously inflexible area of my body and my mind.

Yoga has taught me to slow down and take a step aside from this crazy, fast-paced world, and to pay attention to what is happening right here and now. To be *mindful* puts me in touch with a calm place deep inside me—a calm place that is deep inside all of us.

My experience tells me that yoga works; in addition, of course, to all the scientific evidence and what I've directly observed and heard from my many students I have taught for the past 30 years. It is my experience that has made me believe in yoga, and not any preconceptions or misconceptions.

What Yoga Is Not

It has been my observation that many in the general public and in the medical field have little appreciation of all that yoga has to offer. While this may be changing, I believe many people who could benefit from yoga, shy away due to misconceptions about what yoga is or is not, and who can do yoga or who can't. So, before I go more deeply into the matter of what yoga is, and how it can benefit you, I will address some of these misconceptions:

- Some people avoid yoga because they think it is only for the flexible, strong, and athletic person. If you look at pictures in magazines, or sample some vigorous yoga classes, you could get discouraged. However, there are yoga classes for all types of fitness and ages. Different aspects of yoga would be emphasized; for example, there is gentle yoga and yoga for beginners, and there are props that can be used to assist in many classes.

- Another misconception is that yoga is only for those that are young or in good health. There are people in their 60s, 70s, and beyond doing yoga. I am convinced that if you embrace the practice, you'll increase your odds of going, and you will feel good when you get there. I have had the good fortune of meeting and attending some workshops with one of the great pioneers of introducing yoga to North America, Lilas Folan. She has authored several yoga books and was writing and teaching well into her late 70s. I have personally taught people at all levels of physical fitness and ages—old people, stiff people, people in pain, and people recovering from major illnesses. I believe yoga is continuing to gain acceptance with the medical establishment, as these kinds of people tell me that yoga was suggested to them by their doctor. The best place to start is where you are at. Seek medical approval. Yoga can be modified—for example, chair yoga. And you may be advised not to do some poses, but that's okay!

- Yoga is not a religion. As a Christian, I wondered myself how yoga fit in with my Christian upbringing. As I began to better understand yoga concepts, and truths became more important to my own experience, answers would arrive. Although yoga has long been associated with the Hindu religious tradition, it is not a form of Hinduism. The fact is that yoga is practiced by Christians, Muslims, Jews, Buddhists, atheists, etc. There is a spiritual side to yoga that you can choose to focus on or not. Yoga is compatible with any religion, or none, if that is your preference. A yoga practice allows you the opportunity to take what is important and useful to you and ignore the rest if you choose. For example, while many people find meditation beneficial, it may seem unfamiliar to you, so don't do it. Or chanting "OM" may feel uncomfortable, so chant something else, like a prayer to Jesus, or a prayer for world peace, or don't chant at all.

- And finally, yoga is not about assuming any set of beliefs; it is about coming to know yourself through your own experience. It is not about blindly following anyone but is about assisting you on your chosen path.

How Yoga Can Help

- As the meaning of the word *yoga is* "union," yoga first seeks to unite your body and mind, because what is happening on the outside reflects what is going on with every system inside your body. Often, people separate their minds from their bodies. Some people are not grounded. They can't feel their feet on the ground below. But also, they are not able to cope with the ordinary pressures of daily life, and they collapse. As a result, when people are not fully "in their body," they tend to be somewhat disconnected from the world around them. This can lead to avoidance, rather than facing life's challenges. Through yoga, you are taught to become aware of your body and to be present and mindful in everything you do. This enables you to reconnect your mind and emotions to the body, enabling you to live life more fully and with enjoyment.

- With a yoga practice, you are developing physical, mental, and spiritual "muscles," in a way that can make you happier, less anxious, and more at peace with yourself and the world around you.

- When practicing yoga, you are strengthening and calming the nervous system. With the postures, you are increasing blood flow to the internal organs; and through the breathing exercises, you are bringing more oxygen to your cells. This can allow for more clearing of the mental clutter, allowing you to see things more clearly.

- Yoga asks us to treat our bodies as our temple. And as the quote at the beginning of the chapter states: "Health is wealth ...." You could have all the money and time in the world, but if you don't have your health to enjoy it, it means very little. Yoga encourages us to take responsibility for our own health, with proper exercise, diet, sleep, and managing our stresses. There are so many benefits that yoga can offer the body, but yoga also trains the mind through focusing and meditation. Yoga also examines the body-mind connection and the causes of ill health. These causes are often found to begin in the mind. One of the principle studies in yoga is self-understanding. In yoga, we look at our thoughts and how these mental attitudes shape our behaviors. With knowledge, there is power—the power to make choices to free ourselves from stress and tension.

- While yoga is body and mind training, yoga also tells us that there is something greater beyond the body and mind. It is what we call *spirit*. When I define the word *yoga* as union, I refer to union of the body, mind, and spirit. Also, the greeting of "Namaste" means, "I acknowledge the Divine within you."

- Yoga is much about *balance*. Many people have the impression that the physical practice of yoga is about flexibility but being physically flexible is not the main goal of a yoga practice. It is about *balance*, and not just *physical balance* but *mind and emotional balance.* Everything in you must be balanced and in harmony for you to achieve optimum health. What yoga does is challenge you wherever you need it. It is a process of transferring your weakness into strengths, making you a more *balanced* person. For example, some people come to class very flexible but lack strength. Or there is the opposite, where they are very strong but not flexible. Some people can't relax.

- An imbalanced body can easily influence your emotions and thoughts negatively. A conflicted mind will sooner or later cause, or show up as, physical problems. Yoga helps you bring balance to your body and mind.

A gracious yet simple pose in yoga, called *the Tree* pose, is symbolic of how yoga can bring balance into your life. The pose is meant to bring balance and promote inner stillness. Sometimes trees have to navigate obstacles when growing. Notice how a tree balances itself. It will grow a branch in the opposite direction in which it may be forced to lean. In this posture, you stand still like a tree, and adjust your weight to be perfectly balanced. Yoga helps you apply this principle of balance to your life. Whenever your day-to-day demands are too overwhelming, and you are forced to "bend" to one side, your inner strength and wisdom will serve as counterweights to keep you in balance and able to manage these challenges with perspective. Just as the tree, you cannot be uprooted!

For more details on how yoga postures are symbolic and awaken your body's inner strength and inner wisdom, keep reading ahead until you get to the chapter on beginner-friendly poses. But first learn how to breathe, in the next chapter!

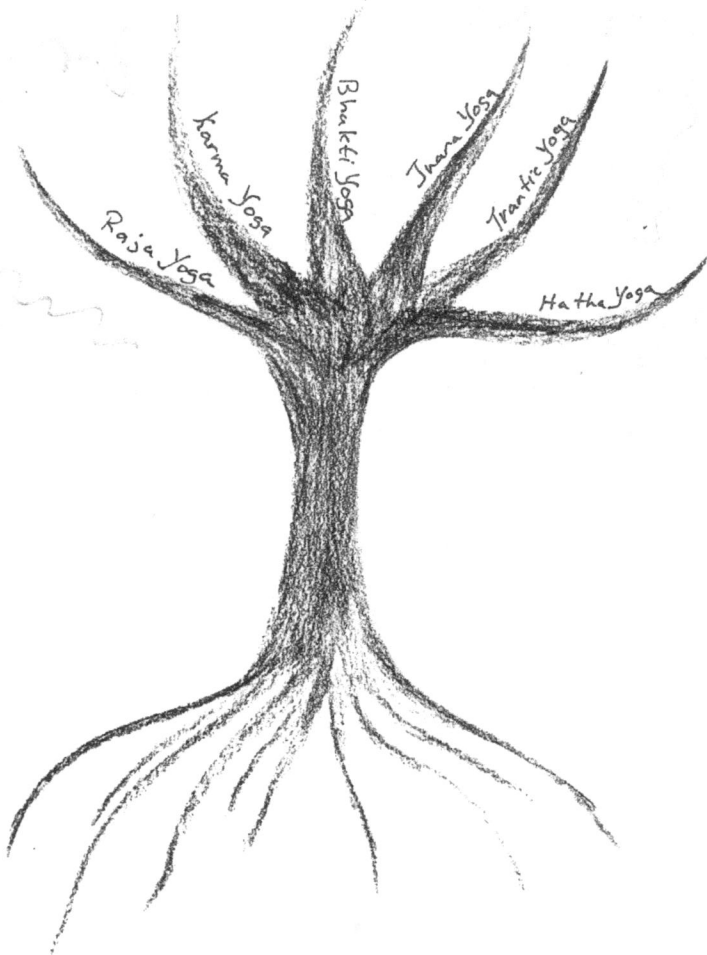

Karma Yoga

Bhakti Yoga

Jnana Yoga

Tantric Yoga

Raja Yoga

Hatha Yoga

Yoga Tree and the 6 Branches of Yoga

Notes

Notes

_____

_____

_____

_____

_____

_____

_____

_____

_____

_____

_____

_____

_____

_____

Chapter Three

Learn How to "Deep Breathe"
Your Stress Away

*"When the breath wanders, the mind is also unsteady.
But when the breath is calmed, the mind too will be still,
and the yogi achieves a long life. Therefore, one
should learn to control the breath."*
– Hatha Yoga Pradipika

In the ancient Sanskrit language, the word for breath is *prana,* which means life energy. The Master of Yoga discovered the usefulness of the breath thousands of years ago. In yoga, the conscious control of breathing is called *pranayama*. In this chapter, I will share their "secrets" with some basic yogic breathing exercises, and how yoga can help alleviate stress through the simple practice of yogic breathing.

The Importance of Oxygen and How the Lungs Work

Oxygen is a component of such immense importance that without it, life would impossible. Most people can live a few weeks without food. They can live a few days without water. But they can only live a few minutes without oxygen. While reading this book, you are probably not even consciously aware that your chest is softly, rhythmically and automatically rising and falling as air enters and exits your lungs. Yet without this intake of air, which contains oxygen, your physical life would end. Within a few minutes, you would quickly become aware of the need for oxygen.

At birth, a child's first and most basic need is to breathe. As soon as the baby's first breath is met with oxygen, immediately we see the chest start to rise and fall, rhythmically and automatically. Breathing in oxygen and exhaling carbon-dioxide begins and continues for the rest of their life.

There are many references in the Bible, of God "breathing" life into us. For example, "the breath of life" that God breathed into Adam at the time of creation.

When we breathe, we take in oxygen through our lungs, which is then placed into our bloodstream. The blood then transports the oxygen, which eventually nourishes and repairs the body's cells. Healthy cells equal a healthy body. The quality of air we breathe, the quality of foods we eat, along with proper exercise and the efficiency of the body to eliminate unnecessary waste, all contribute to the health of our cells. Breathing clean, fresh air increases the quality and length of our lives. Also, the way we breathe, most commonly being shallow/chest breathing, does not efficiently oxygenate blood that is circulating in your arteries and veins. With a decrease in the supply of oxygen to the cells, toxins build up. As toxins build up, the body becomes physically, mentally, and emotionally sluggish and tired, with the eventual breakdown of the organs.

With a decrease in the supply of oxygen to the brain, the brain's mental abilities will result in poor thought processes, and the ability to make good decisions is diminished. With an increase in the supply of oxygen, the brain's mental abilities increase. The brain becomes more alert. With an increase in the supply of oxygen to the body's cells, the body becomes more alive and full of energy and life. And with the increase in oxygen, we become more optimistic and better ready to handle life's challenges, mentally and emotionally. Sickness and disease cannot survive in a well-oxygenated body. If you take the word *disease* apart, you have "dis" and "ease." Let yoga help you get back to "ease" in life.

Alleviate Stress Through the Simple Practice of Yogic Breathing

In yoga, we use the breath to move in and out of a posture. This allows us to relax and to achieve the deepest possible effect from the posture.

We use breath control, called *pranayama,* to "awaken" life energy, called *prana,* which is stored in our body to increase our vitality. Also, by consciously directing our breath and breathing into a particular part or organ in our body, we can remove energetic blockages and facilitate healing. Like acupuncture or reflexology, where there are lines of energy throughout the body, ill health occurs when these lines of energy are blocked. This also helps strengthen our immune system.

Yogic breathing is calming, clearing, and quieting to the mind. (I am referring to that inner voice that seems to be constantly chattering.) It allows for the opportunity of better control of our emotions—anxiety, fear, anger, and pain.

You may notice that when you calm your nervous system, you can positively influence the nervousness and nervous energy of the people around you. In my career as a probation and parole officer, I have worked with people who were in conflict with the law. Many of these people were struggling with addictions and mental health issues. Often, they were anxious and angry with their life's circumstances. I would observe their breathing, and it was most often shallow (high in the chest) and erratic. I would purposefully slow down my own breathing as I listened to the person's story. It would take a few minutes, but this simple breathing technique helped me stay cool and calm and would often influence the other person to calm down.

The practice of conscious breathing improves concentration. I have been told by my yoga teacher that there are three steps to meditation. The first is to be able to relax the body; the second step is to be able to concentrate, and then you can meditate. To learn what these yoga breathing techniques are, read on!!

Yogic Breathing Techniques

I am now going to introduce you to three specific yoga breathing techniques: the *three-part yogic breath, alternate nostril breathing, and the breath of joy.*

Before you learn about these various techniques, I want you to take a few minutes and review some tips about breathing in general, which can help you enjoy your experience more fully.

• Keep your jaw, tongue, and facial muscles relaxed, and shoulders down from your ears, and your spine elongated.

• Be aware of any clothing that may constrict breathing, for example, belts.

• Don't overdo the number of repetitions, and don't strain your breathing; remain relaxed while you do the breathing exercises. Relaxation invites proper breathing.

• I was a lifeguard and swim instructor for many years. Similar to breathing while swimming, one must exhale completely before inhaling.

• Yogic breathing is typically done through the nose, both during inhalation and exhalation. The yoga masters believed the mouth was for eating and the nose for breathing. By breathing through the nose, the air is filtered, and the breath is slowed down. (Slow is good in yoga!)

Note: As yoga is "flexible," there are always exceptions to these "rules." There may be certain physiological conditions that prevent you from breathing through your nose. Also, if lying down to practice is difficult, sit up. It may help to inhale through the nose and exhale through the mouth. And if you need to, just breathe through your mouth and don't worry for now. Also, there are a few classical yogic breathing exercises where you do breathe through your mouth.

- And finally, just take the time to relax throughout the day, and *JUST BREATHE!* I would often, between appointments, take a *breather* sometime through the day. Because of the necessity for confidentiality with the clientele I worked with, I had my own office. I would close the door and sit quietly for a few moments and *just breathe.* Many yoga breathing techniques can be done sitting wherever you happen to be. I found that by taking a simple *breathing pause,* it made me feel *refreshed.*

Before you jump right in and make drastic changes to your method of breathing, take a few minutes, and watch and observe your breathing patterns. Do not judge yourself. Be only, as we say in yoga, the "witness." You may wish to ask yourself: Do I easily get out of breath? Is my breathing shallow? Are my inhalations and exhalations steady? How is my breathing pattern when something is upsetting or stressful in my life? Now think about how many times you've heard someone say, "N*ow take a few deep breaths and relax."* This recommendation is so popular because IT WORKS!!

The following breathing techniques will show you how to breathe deeply and calm your nervous system, as well as show you how the breath is used to move "through" a posture.

The Three-Part Yogic Breath

The three-part yogic breath is one of the simplest and most beneficial of all yoga exercises. Its name comes from the movement of the diaphragm, the rib cage, and the upper chest.

Benefits:

- The three-part breath "massages" inner organs such as the lungs, diaphragm, and abdominal muscles.

- This way of breathing uses all your lung capacity, bringing more oxygen and life prana into your system.

- This way of breathing moves the spine, and the chest widens. It helps restore "flexibility" and function of the organs in your chest and abdomen.

- It can stimulate digestion.

- This deep breathing also reaches down into your "gut" emotions. It was not uncommon for my students to experience sighs and even a few tears as the emotional tension was released in the body. (Instead of feeling embarrassed, I would encourage my students to rejoice in their newfound inner freedom.)

- Whenever you feel tired, depressed, or discouraged, do this breathing; it can make you feel refreshed and revitalized.

How to Do:

- Lie on your back with knees bent and feet flat on the floor

- Place one hand on your chest, the other on your abdomen.

- Begin the inhalation by expanding the belly (feel your belly moving against your hand and upward); keep the chest motionless if possible, in this (part one).

- Continue the inhalation, expanding the lower rib cage (part two).

- And finally, feel the inhalation in the chest as it rises (part three).

- Exhale while releasing the chest, ribcage, and lastly, the abdomen.

Make sure you try and pause between the inhalations and exhalations. If you feel dizzy, short of breath, or are straining to breathe, stop! Once finished a few rounds of this breathing technique, return to your everyday breathing, but enjoy the quiet within.

Note: This breathing technique can be done sitting or standing (and should be done all the time!). It is easiest to demonstrate lying down, and to feel the movement of the three parts.

Alternate Nostril Breathing

Yoga masters have known for hundreds of years that we don't breathe evenly through both nostrils. Yoga is all about balance and awareness within the body. Alternate nostril breathing is believed to balance the sympathetic and parasympathetic branches of the nervous system. For myself, the onset of a head cold is often experienced with one nostril becoming "blocked" (time to get my neti pot out). Or it is a sign that my mind needs a break from all that thinking, or I need some emotional balance.

How to Do:

- Sit comfortably on the floor or on a chair, with your spine elongated, and your left hand on your lap.

- With your right hand, make a fist. Release your little and ring finger from the fist. The thumb remains over the middle and index finger.

- Place your right hand in front of you (in the center of your body) so that your thumb closes the right nostril (just touch the side of your nostril). Your ring finger will close the left nostril.

- With your thumb, close the right nostril and slowly inhale through your left nostril.

- As soon as you finish inhaling, close the left nostril and exhale through your right nostril. At the end of the exhalation, inhale back through the right nostril.

- Next, close the right nostril and exhale through the left. At the end of the exhalation, inhale through the left nostril, the same nostril through which you just exhaled.

- Continue to breathe in this pattern, keeping the body relaxed and the breath flowing easily.

Do this initially for a minute or so. You may want to mentally count to a number (3) on the inhale and use the same number as you exhale. Over time, you will find your breath moving toward a 1-4-2 ratio. This means if you are inhaling to the count of 3, you hold the breath (both nostrils are closed now) to a count of 12, and exhale to a count of 6.

Once you have completed your session, sit quietly, close your eyes, and become aware of the still, peaceful place within.

The Breath of Joy

This breath combines deep breathing with fluid motion.

Benefits:

This is an energizing warm-up that uses the rhythmic motion of the body to encourage deep breathing. The arm motion in this exercise facilitates filling the lower, middle, and then upper lungs.

How to Do:

- Stand with your feet hip-width apart, knees slightly flexed, or as I prefer to say, keep the back of your knees "soft" to protect the lower back.

- As you begin to inhale, raise your arms in front of you to shoulder height.

- Next, "sweep" the arms out to the sides (shoulder height) and complete your inhalation as you raise your arms over your head, palms facing toward each other.

- "Swing" the arms toward the ground as you bend forward on your exhalation, exhaling the breath out with a "ha" sound.

- Bend forward from the hips and let the motion (momentum) of the movement carry your arms behind you. Emphasize the breath, letting the motion be smooth and unforced. Inhalations, as you raise your arms, are a short "sniff" with each movement. For example, raise your arms to shoulder height (short, quick sniff); raise your arms out to the side (short, quick sniff); and then raise your arms above your head (short, quick sniff).

- Do a few rounds and feel the newfound energy and joy in the body!

Breathing Your Way into Postures

Yoga postures are best performed in co-ordination with movement of the breath. As you practice conscious breathing and yoga postures, you will notice that the flow of the breath (inhalations and exhalations) naturally inspires and initiates movement. For example, in a back bend, the chest and belly "open" to allow the breath to naturally flow in (inhalation). As you fold into a forward bend, the breath naturally flows out (exhalation) as you bend forward. More on this topic is found in the chapters ahead. Read on!!

Continue to breathe deeply and make it a habit. Let me show you the way, in the upcoming chapter, with some friendly yoga poses. But first let me explain the importance of "warming up" before stretching.

Notes

_____

_____

_____

_____

_____

_____

_____

_____

_____

_____

_____

_____

_____

_____

Notes

_____

_____

_____

_____

_____

_____

_____

_____

_____

_____

_____

_____

_____

Chapter Four

Warm Up Before Stretching

"You are created to excel. There's no limit to how high you can go in life. Keep stretching to the next level."
– Joel Osteen

Why Warm Up?

Most people believe that stretching should come before their warm-up when exercising. And because many people think of yoga just as a type of stretching, they have mistakenly or erroneously been misinformed as to the benefits of warming up before starting a yoga practice. Many people think that as they are moving and using their muscles during the workout, they do not need to stretch before moving; however, warming up is necessary to protect the muscles.

There are numerous reasons to warm-up prior to stretching:

- You can view "warming up" in the literal sense: You are increasing the temperature of your muscles before stretching, to prevent straining them.

- Warming up prior to stretching acts to loosen muscular connecting tissue, and releases tension.

- Warm-ups are designed to enhance overall flexibility. They also increase circulation throughout your body, thus bringing more oxygen into your muscles.

- The practice of warming up also functions to flood your heart with plenty of oxygen to reduce the overall stress placed on your heart while working out.

- Making sure you warm up your body before you stretch will better your range of motion and will allow you to move more easily while reducing your risk of injury and lessening the possibility of developing cramps.

- Warm-ups assist muscles and *"fascia"* to be released in a creative, non-aggressive way.

What Is Fascia, and Why Is It Important to Warm Up?

Fascia is everywhere in the body; it holds us together. It is a fiber-gel connective tissue that surrounds and holds your body— every muscle, every organ, and every blood vessel.

- Fascia facilitates every movement of your body. It enables your muscles to move over and around organs without resistance.

- Fascia allows individual muscles to lengthen and shorten. The fascial system maintains a balance of tension and elasticity, which allows for smoother movement of each muscle group while holding everything together.

- If fascia is restricted, then muscle contraction is restricted. Restriction is where pain and injury can happen. Stress, toxins, inactivity, and excessive activity affect fascia. I believe that even powerful emotions and thoughts can possibly settle deep into the fascia.

- Fascia consistency changes with age. It begins to lose resiliency as we age. It is especially important to warm up the fascia as we get older.

When healthy, fascia is flexible, supple, tough, and fibrous, and is best warmed up slowly. Yoga helps stretch and ease the fiber webbing, as well as hydrate the gel. Over time, with a yoga practice, fascial fiber will slowly thin out and change to a more liquid state, allowing more "gliding," with less pain, more feeling, and less resistance. Yoga is a great tool to get fluids moving!

How to Improve Fascia Health

There are many ways of warming up fascia:

- Self-massage: "tapping," "thumping," and forming a "cup" with your hand, can be used to help muscle fibers to warm up or release their tightness. Tapping is used for toning small muscles such as those in the face. It is a light tap using the fingertips. Thumping is done using the sides of the hands but with the hands lightly clenched. You can massage either side of the spine, up and down the back. Form a cup with your hands by having them clenched, as in thumping, but instead of using the sides of your hand, form a "cup" with them as you tap along the arms, shoulders, and legs, from the hips to the ankles. With this type of massage, you would use one hand to tap along the opposite arm, or shoulder, neck, etc.

- To help warm up the buttock and hamstring muscles, one of my favorite exercises is what I call "run the mat." Begin by sitting at one end of your mat with straight legs. Bend your arms in a motion as if you were running. Now, on your butt, begin to jog, rolling from one leg/side to the other as you run on your butt to the end of your mat and back again.

- Another excellent warm-up for shoulders, back, and arms is what I call "rock and roll." Try this technique by beginning in a seated position on the floor. Bring the soles of your feet together and take hold of your ankles. In one continuous motion, first roll onto one shoulder, then to your back, and come up on the opposite shoulder.

Awaken the Feet

Being a certified reflexologist, I often have my yoga students do some *reflexology* on their feet, as part of warming up. *Reflexology* is based on the theory that the body's energy channels can be unblocked, stimulated, and revitalized through certain reflex points on the feet.

Stress and negative emotions restrict the flow of energy around the body. Under stress, the healthy blood and nerve supply to organs is constricted, which starves the tissues and organs, and leads to a rise in toxins and an increased risk of illness.

Relaxation is the key during treatment as both feet are worked on. These treatments affect a person as a whole, raising inner vitality. Stress-related conditions respond well to reflexology. Responsible reflexology is never completely contraindicated because it is deceptively powerful; thus, I would advise seeking out a certified reflexologist for a professional session.

Respect the Body's Need to Warm Up

Taking the time to warm up results in a more enjoyable, safe, and beneficial yoga experience. Warming up honors your body's need to move gradually into movement and deeper stretching. If you don't begin your practice slowly, increasing the intensity of your stretches, you risk injury. Warm-ups can be done either on the floor or standing, but the key is to gently work the whole body with repetitive movements that do not require a lot of exertion or stretching to your full range of motion.

There are no absolute rules for warm-ups or warm-up times. Remember, the warm-ups are assisting muscles and fascia to release in non-aggressive ways. And at the end of your warm-ups, you should feel more alert, coordinated, and physically warm. Your breathing will be deeper, and your eyesight should sharpen. You will not feel tired but more alive!

How to Begin Your Yoga Practice

When you first begin your yoga practice, take a few moments to transition from the business of your "outer" world. I begin my classes with a short relaxation before warming up. The following is an example of this short relaxation that I begin with. (A longer relaxation is done at the end of a class.) It is a time to physically relax and to mentally let go of the busyness of your world. After this transition, you are ready to move into your warm-ups.

Short Relaxation:

- Lie down on your mat, eyes closed.

- Bring your awareness down to your feet, your toes. Stretch them, and tighten your legs while inhaling; then hold, and on an exhalation, *let go* of the tension from your legs, feet, and toes.

- Bring your awareness to your buttocks, arms, and shoulders; inhale, squeeze, tense up, and exhale, and then *let go, and relax.*

- Gently roll your head side to side; let it find its own center. *Relax* the neck.

- Make a "face" by squeezing your cheeks; squint your eyes and *let go—relaxing* all your facial muscles.

- And finally, to quiet the mind, begin to follow your breath as you inhale and exhale; and with every exhalation, *let go* of all tension and worries.

Now allow these relaxing movements guide you into your warm-ups. Rest quietly for a minute or two longer. Now you are ready to move into your warm-ups and preparation for the *asanas* (yoga postures). There are no rules for warm-up time, but in my hour-long class, I spend about 10 minutes warming up, and have a short relaxation.

To warm up the big muscle groups of the body, quickly and enjoyably, instead of holding a stretch, we add movement. The following are examples of movement while warming up:

- Spinal Rock and Roll – While lying on the floor, draw your knees to your chest and "hug" your knees. Simply rock and roll from one side of your spine to the other (left/right and back). You are massaging the lower, middle, and upper back, as well as the shoulders. Rock over even further, side to side, and massage the upper back of your arms, the back of your neck, and your head.

- Spinal Twists – Remaining lying down, keep knees bent and place your feet on the floor, hip-width apart. Extend arms, shoulder height, out to the sides. Keep your shoulders and arms on the ground. Drop your knees toward one side, while at the same time, roll your head to the opposite side. Repeat a few times on either side.

- Half Bridge Pose – Go back to center, with knees and feet hip-width apart. Gently press lower back toward the floor. Without moving your head, slowly begin to lift hips toward the ceiling, coming into a Half Bridge pose. Hold, squeezing the thigh muscles, and slowly lower your hips to the floor. Let the lower back "sink" into the floor, and gently roll your head side to side to release any tension in the neck. Draw knees to your chest and lift head to touch knees (if possible). Place your head down, and with feet now on the floor, roll over to your right side and come up to a seated position.

Seven Warm-up Exercises

The following exercises are great warm-ups and stretches that prepare the body and mind before beginning your routine. Each exercise targets different parts of the body.

Spinal Warm-Up

Benefit: It has been noted by many yoga masters that you are as young as your spine is flexible. This stretch specifically targets the spine by systematically warming it from the base upward.

How to Do:

- Start by sitting on the floor, with crossed legs. Straighten the spine by pressing the chest slightly forward and lifting the rib cage. Relax the shoulders and slightly tuck the chin.

- Inhale and flex the spine forward, chest out and shoulders back.

- Exhale and slump the body, round the shoulders forward. The head will come forward but focus on rounding the spine.

- Inhale as you lift the chest, bringing the chin level with the floor; relax the shoulders, sit tall, and repeat the exercise 3 to 5 times.

Neck Tilts

Benefit: If you are like me, a great deal of your tension is carried in your neck and shoulders. This is a favorite warm-up of mine because I can immediately feel release. It is an exercise that can be done anywhere and anytime, such as during an hourly break from the computer. By stretching and lengthening the neck muscles, this exercise helps the whole body to relax, and quiets the mind.

How to Do:

- Sit or stand tall with shoulders down from the ears. Tilt your head to the right side, and rather than bringing your ear to your shoulder, consciously extend and elongate your neck.

- At the same time, press your left hand into the floor. *Hold, breathe, and relax!* Repeat on the opposite side.

Chest Expanders

Benefits: This warm-up can be done standing or sitting. This stretch breaks up muscle tension and stress carried within the muscles of your torso. It improves posture and breathing. This is another exercise that can be done at your desk. Take a timeout from the computer and do the chest expander exercise on a coffee break. It energizes and clears the brain.

How to Do:

- Begin by rolling the shoulders in slow, large circles in both directions, maybe 3 times forward and 3 times backwards.

- Next, clasp your hands behind you or use a belt to hold onto.

- Standing or sitting tall, roll your shoulders back and down. Straighten your elbows, lifting your arms upward. Feel the chest open and expand.

- Now, *relax,* and re-stretch (2–3 times).

Cat and Dog Stretch

Benefits: This warm-up stretch promotes both flexibility and strength in the arms and back. It also allows for the organs in the torso to "fall" back into place and gives the heart a rest. This stretch is an excellent release for lower back stiffness.

How to Do:

- Begin in Table pose: Kneeling on all fours, place hands directly under your shoulders, with knees under hips. The spine is neutral.

- Inhale, and lift your chin and tailbone upwards, arching the spine like a "saddle" in your back.

- Exhale and round the spine, lifting your navel up while moving your head and tailbone down.

- Repeat exercise 3–5 times.

Bound Angle Pose – Baddha Konasana **(Sanskrit name *Baddha* means "bound," and *Kona* means "angle")**

Benefits: This warm-up is one of the best hip openers around. It counter acts "chair" hips. If you have a job like mine, you spend most of your day sitting at a desk.

How to Do:

- Sit on the floor, with legs straight out in front of you; raise your pelvis with a blanket if your hips or groin are tight.

- On an exhalation, bend your knees and pull your heels toward your pelvis; then drop your knees out to the sides.

- Press the soles of your feet together.

* Hold, breathe, and relax. Repeat.

Half Moon Pose – *Ardha Chandrasana* (Sanskrit name *Ardha* means "half," and *Chandra* means "moon")

Benefits: The Half Moon pose addresses lateral flexion of the spine and is preparatory to all sideward stretches.

How to Do:

- Stand in Mountain pose: Feet together, toes pointing forward, and arms at your sides; relax your shoulders, and keep your chin parallel to the floor.

- Inhaling raise your hands toward the ceiling, palms facing each other and shoulder width apart above your head.

- Exhaling, stretch and press and lift your left hip and rib cage to the left. At the same time, lean your body to the right, into a crescent moon shape. Relax the shoulders.

- Come back to center and repeat on the other side.

Downward Facing Dog – *Adho Mukha Svanasana* (Sanskrit name *Adho* means "down," *Mukha* means "face," and *Svana* means "dog")

Benefits: This pose has many benefits; it elongates the spine and stretches the muscles of the arms, legs, and back. It is also a great upper body strengthener, as well as being energizing.

How to Do:

- From Table pose, spread fingers wide apart and curl toes under.

- Take a deep breath in. Exhale as you press into your hands and balls of your feet to lift the hips up.

- Keep the knees bent, the spine straight, and the neck long.

- *HOLD, BREATHE, RELAX, and REST.*

Now that you have the knowledge on how to breathe efficiently and properly warm up, let's get into yoga poses that will help you release tension and stress—this and more, in the next chapter!!

Notes

_____

_____

_____

_____

_____

_____

_____

_____

_____

_____

_____

_____

_____

_____

Chapter Five

Eight Beginner-Friendly Yoga Poses
That Awaken Your Inner Wisdom

*"It doesn't matter how deep into a posture you go;
what matters is who you are when you get there."*
– Max Strom

The Essence of a Pose

When most people think of yoga, they think of yoga asanas or postures. And they think of them as a form of exercise. Students tell me that the most common reason they have for taking a class is that they are either seeking relief from some physical discomfort, or that they want to learn how to relax. Few people, especially when beginning, express an interest in the emotional or spiritual aspects of yoga, and that is perfectly fine! However, those who stay with the practice will discover, as I mentioned previously, that their practice will evolve, and certain discoveries will unfold. You will feel better physically, and eventually you begin to breathe more freely without effort. Concentration and focus improve as your state of mind changes. With that shift, you become more alert and alive. And then something else is "awakened" in you—the sense that there is something beyond the body/mind aspect of yourself. You will soon become aware that each asana offers certain physical, psychological, and spiritual benefits. Each asana allows for a certain meditative state of mind.

These postures correctly mirror our bodies' design, so that when properly practiced, they bring about the full potential and natural range of movement in the human body. All the bending, twisting, and turning promotes the efficient functioning of our internal organs and helps balance the sympathetic and parasympathetic nervous systems. The effect of the practice of the asanas on the central nervous system cannot be ignored. Through a continued practice, students develop a greater awareness of what is going on inside them. This allows for optimal health and well-being. Yoga recognizes the body and mind connection, and the potential of them working together.

As your practice continues, you will discover that yoga is not limited to just the physical. It begins there because our awareness is physical. The practice of yoga will lead to increasing self-knowledge (who you really are). This newfound knowledge means that you can control not only your physical body but your mind. For example, you will become aware of the stresses in the body, and by use of your mind, changes can be made to alleviate them. These changes are now made by conscious decisions, on the basis that you now have choices. An excellent way to develop this awareness is by taking time to reflect and *SLOW DOWN!* The inability to cope with stress and the feelings of hopelessness and helplessness that many people experience, can be counteracted by recognizing that you have options, and by applying the power of choice within yourself. Once you are proficient at a pose, it is then that this awareness flows into every cell and fiber of the body. It is then that you experience the unitedness of your body and your true self. For those of us wanting to find a deeper meaning in the asanas, psychologically and spiritually, one can investigate the postures as symbols and find in them a "hidden wisdom" (more on this later in the chapter).

Some Tips Before Beginning Your Yoga Practice

- Whatever shape you are in right now is the perfect place to begin your practice. Yoga begins with *accepting yourself,* wherever you are at, and celebrating your strengths and acknowledging your limitations. I have learned to be *patient;* the body will move and change when it is ready. You must learn to *listen* to your body and acknowledge its *inner wisdom.*

- Learn to *appreciate* your own experience and *let go* of the natural tendency to compare yourself to the person next to you, or even worse, compare yourself to a photograph in any book. Many people get discouraged when they see photos of people doing advanced poses. They don't consider that perhaps these models have practiced for several years, or that they are double-jointed or gymnasts. These advanced poses look great and desirable, but their health benefits are the same as the handful or so of fundamental postures that make up most students' daily routines. You are about to learn some of these fundamental poses. They are coming up soon, so keep reading.

- Focus on your actual moment-to-moment experience, which is really the only thing that matters. Strive to be *present,* not perfect. In one of my children's classes, we had a saying: "Practice is perfect!"

- Go at your own pace, without pushing yourself or risking injury. There is no place in yoga for the motto of "no pain, no gain." *Respect* your body.

- I recommend that when beginning to practice yoga, you attend classes taught by a certified yoga instructor. They will have the training to guide you through the do's and do nots.

The Asanas

To further clarify the word *asana*, it is the Sanskrit word, meaning "posture." Originally, the word meant a sitting pose for meditation; and later, in Hatha yoga, the meaning included poses for standing, inversions, balances, and twists.

I have heard that there are over 700,000 yoga poses. Many of them require great strength and flexibility. But for centuries, yoga masters have been content with just a handful of practices. In my own yoga classes, I follow a traditional sequencing of practices that tend to "flow" and are a "balanced" mix of movements. These movements are postures that stretch or move the spine and body in different directions—seven directions actually—forward/backward, side to side, up/down, and finally, stillness. Some of these postures in the practice are used as warm-ups; others focus on strengthening core muscles that support proper alignment in the body. Every class of mine includes backbends, lateral stretches to both sides, and twists that rotate the vertebrae of the spine. There is always some sort of an inversion, along with relaxation exercises and breathing exercises.

Asanas are usually named in groups: animals, plants, birds, and structures. The name of the *asana* is the place to begin looking for its symbolic meaning and may evoke in you self-discovery and insights (your inner wisdom).

Mountain Pose – *Tadasana* (*Tada* means "mountain")

This asana is the foundation of all standing poses.

Benefits:

- Improves posture, and strengthens knees, thighs, and ankles

- Inspires increased awareness of the body/mind connections

- Helps decrease anxiety through focused breathing

How to Do:

- In this pose, the body is as steady and still as a mountain. The weight is evenly distributed on the feet, and arms are relaxed at your sides. The spine is elongated, and the back of the neck is straight. Chin is level with the floor.

- Stand with your feet hip-width apart, and arms at your sides.

- Elongate the spine by lifting the chest. Stabilize your core by pressing the tailbone down.

- Relax the shoulders down away from the ears. With each inhalation, lengthen up; and with each exhalation, *relax* the body.

Inner Wisdom:

- When you look at a mountain, what comes to mind? Perhaps standing tall?

- What insights are brought to mind? Standing tall and upright requires strength, awareness of your body, and concentration. There may be the urge to want to move; stillness and swaying must be conquered to remain in this pose.

- Stillness can cultivate space for the body to *pause and rest*.

Tree Pose – *Vrikshasana* (*Vriksha* means "tree")

One of the attitudes worth cultivating is *balance* in your everyday life. Yoga helps your body in an overall more balanced way—left to right, front to back—which can help minimize the muscle imbalance that often leads to one side of the body being stronger.

Benefits:

- Improves balance and stability in the legs

- Strengthens the entire standing leg (thighs, calves, ankles, and spine)

- Strengthens the bones of the hips

How to Do:

- Standing tall in Mountain pose, shift your weight onto the left foot. Bring your gaze to rest at a point in front of you, either on a wall or the floor.

- your right foot, bringing the sole of the foot to rest on the ankle, calf, or inner thigh of the standing leg.

- Use your hands as needed to assist in positioning the foot; then bring them into prayer position.

- Inhale and sweep the arms out to the sides and over your head. *Relax* the upper shoulders, upper back, and neck. *Breathe* deeply as you hold the pose.

Inner Wisdom:

- When you look at a tree, what comes to mind? The alignment, the uprightness, the strength? Trees can hold themselves upright. The Tree pose can be thought of as building self-confidence and self-esteem

• There is a balance between the branches of the tree and the root system, which expands in width and length. A balanced attitude in all aspects of life can help overcome or avoid stress.

Downward Dog – *Adho Mukha Svanasana* (*Adho* means "down," *Mukha* means "face," *Svana* means "dog," and *Asana* means "pose")

The pose is a forward bend named after the resemblance to a dog stretching.

Benefits:

• Improves your mood by bringing more oxygen to the brain

• Improves blood circulation

• Improves digestion

• Increases energy

• Reduces stress and anxiety

• Full body stretch that lengthens and strengthens your bones and muscles

How to Do:

- Start in Table pose (on all fours, with hands under shoulders, and knees under hips).

- Press hands into floor, and curl toes under.

- Push hips up and back as you straighten your legs.

- Lift up through your tailbone to keep the spine straight.

Inner Wisdom:

- As your feet, hands, and legs are all engaged, it is a very grounding, stabilizing pose for emotions.

- It is very energizing if feeling sluggish.

- It evolves feelings of not only physical strength but mental strength (focus).

Triangle Pose – *Utthita Trikonasana* (*Utthita* means "extended," *Tri* means "three," and *Kona* means "angle")

Triangle poses require focus, concentration, and attention to the breath. This awareness of breath, and total presence in the moment, is the single most powerful tool in releasing tension and stress.

Benefits:

- This pose is a deep stretch for the hamstrings, groins, and hips.

- Triangle pose opens the chest and shoulders, two places where tension lives.

- It helps relieve lower back discomfort.

- It is a neck exercise.

- It strengthens our physical and emotional bodies.

How to Do:

- Step the feet as wide apart as your legs are long.

- Turn your left foot out to a ninety-degree turn. The body stretches to the left, moving from the pelvis and extending over the left leg.

- Both arms are perpendicular to the floor, the left hand on the floor, or on a block.

- The spine is straight, the chest is open, and the body is facing to the front.

Inner Wisdom:

- What comes to mind when you think of a triangle? Some of the qualities might be strength and the ability to support weight and resist pressure. As you stand, you may ask yourself how much you can support and how well you can resist pressure.

- It allows us to bring expansion to the muscles that need it most, and by extending and lengthening, creates space in these places of emotional release and healing.

Seated Forward Bend – *Paschimottanasana* (means "intense stretch to the west")

As forward bends are calming and quieting, you can look inward. This could be an opportunity for releasing into a place of surrender and humility.

Benefits:

- The pose stretches the entire back, from the head to the heels.

- It helps relieve problems with sciatica.

- It massages the internal organs, especially the digestive organs.

- It calms the brain and nervous system and helps relieve stress and fatigue.

How to Do:

- Sit on the floor with legs extended and feet together. Flex feet to engage the muscles of the legs.

- Inhale, and lift the arms out to the sides and overhead, palms facing each other. Relax the shoulders.

- As you exhale, slowly bend forward with the spine elongated. Relax the back of the neck as you continue to extend, leading with the crown of your head.

- To release, bring the hands to rest, palms down, on either side of your legs.

Inner Wisdom:

- The important lesson that this pose teaches is *surrender*. This posture stretches many muscles and ligaments, but everyone has a limit. It also stretches the limitations in one's thinking and understanding. As you bend forward, you cannot see behind or above, and you surrender to this fact. In accepting this situation, lies humility.

- Also, regarding *patience* and *surrender*, we can take time to strengthen and lengthen our attitudes.

Cobra – *Bhujangasana* (*Bhujanga* means "serpent")

Cobra is an energizing backbend that opens the heart for stress reduction and anxiety relief.

Benefits:

- Strengthens and increases flexibility in the spine and shoulders

- Improves digestion by stimulating the abdominal organs

- Helps open the lungs, which is therapeutic for asthma

- Can help improve posture as it counters the slouch that comes from sitting in front of a computer, or from commuting daily with long drives

How to Do:

- Lie on your belly with your forehead on the floor. Place your hands, palms down, under your shoulders, elbows touching the sides of the body.

- Inhale, press through the hands, and begin to lift the head and then your torso by engaging the back muscles. Open the chest and arch the spine back.

- To release, exhale and extend the torso forward and down to the floor.

- Turn the head to one side and bring the arms to the sides with your palms facing up.

Inner Wisdom:

- Snakes must continually shed their skin in order to grow. Perhaps the ability to shed its skin symbolizes renewal. Think of times when we must shed the "old skin" to let the new being emerge. If you have ever seen a snake just after shedding its old skin, the "new" looks shiny, clear, and refreshed.

Shoulder Stand – *Salamba Sarvangasana* (*Salamba* means "with support," *Sarva* means "whole," *Anga* means "body")

The Shoulder Stand is an inversion. All inversions are powerful postures that deserve and demand respect. Having said that, I would recommend that any beginner avoid this until under the guidance of a certified teacher.

Benefits:

- Strengthens neck, upper back, and shoulders

- Strengthens and relaxes the heart and respiratory system

- Combats common colds

- Decreases varicose veins and reduces wrinkles

How to Do:

In my yoga classes, some of the students do Shoulder Stand, but I offer two simple, modified versions of Shoulder Stand, which allows for anyone to experience the power and benefits of this inversion.

- The first modified version involves using a chair. Begin the pose by lying on your back on the floor. Bring your knees to your chest and place the seat side of the chair directly under your knees. Have your arms slightly out from your body. Close your eyes and enjoy!

- The second inversion is simply having your legs up the wall. Sitting near a wall, position your body against the wall with your hip touching. Then bring your knees into your chest; and in one motion, turn your buttocks toward the wall and swing your legs up.

- Come to lie on your back with buttocks touching the wall, and legs extended up.

Inner Wisdom:

- Shoulder Stand makes me think of my shoulders and how much in life I must "shoulder." What responsibilities and burdens do I carry? I believe that God only gives us what we are able to carry on our shoulders.

- I remind myself that Shoulder Stand is just one of many postures I practice, and as such, no one can "stand" on their shoulders forever. As I move into another position, it is just as life is in movement and nothing lasts forever. There is always something changing in your body and in your mind, as well as in your life.

Seated Spinal Twist – *Ardha Matsyendrasana* (*Ardha* means "half," *Matsyendrasana* was a sage who spread the teachings of yoga)

Benefits:

- Strengthens the spine

- Improves flexibility

- Calms the nervous system

- "Wrings" out venous blood and allows oxygenated blood to flow in

How to Do:

- While seated, extend left leg on the floor; bend right leg and lift over the left leg. Place right foot flat on the floor, on the outside of left thigh.

- The body twists to the right; the head looks back over right shoulder.

- Place right hand on floor, behind back.

- Left arm is wrapped around right knee.

Inner Wisdom:

- Just as the body is twisted and constricted like a tied knot, there may be something going on with our emotions and our minds.

- Sometimes the mind can be flexible and able to untwist matters.

In this chapter, I have introduced you to just a few of the many poses of yoga. I have chosen these poses as they move the spine in what I call the seven directions in yoga: left/right, up/down, twist, forward/backward. This is how I would structure my own yoga classes, and of course with breathing and relaxation exercises. I have presented an explanation for each pose, which I hope will help clarify one or two points for both beginner and experienced students, as well as offering a deeper symbolic aspect of the poses, for your own exploration. In any event, I hope to make your practice more interesting, more attractive, and more personal. For a depiction of these eight beginner's poses, see the last page of this chapter.

By now, you probably have realized that we are doing more than learning just a few yoga poses. While you may have been interested in yoga because you felt the need to keep in shape, or you needed to learn how to relax, I know from experience that there is much more to yoga than our physical bodies. In order to practice the postures of yoga to their fullest, we need to be aware of our whole selves. With regular practice, you will strengthen your muscles and can expect to become more flexible. You will learn to be centered in the present moment and will learn about self-acceptance. You will become quieter, and each time you contemplate or reflect, you will be strengthening your will. The asanas have symbolic meanings that you can use as a personal reflection tool. Record these insights (inner wisdom) from your yoga practice and apply them in your daily life.

But as in all exercises, and with all your "muscles"—physical, mental, emotional, and spiritual—you need to "use them or lose them." Read on to the next chapter and find out the importance of daily practice, and some special sequencing of postures to allow your practice to flow naturally.

By the way, my book is not just a book but a book plus a website. I have mentioned so many things thus far; you may just want to go right now, if you have a moment, and see all the wonderful extras you can get. Just go to: thebreatheandrelaxbook.com.

Eight Beginner Friendly Asanas

The asanas are usually named in groups: animals, plants, structures. The name of the asana is the place to begin looking for its symbolic meaning and self-discoveries/inner wisdoms they may evoke.

Explore these fascinating symbols as a personal reflection tool. Which symbols are you drawn to, and why?

Mountain Pose

Triangle Pose

Seated Twist Pose

Shoulder Stand

Downward Dog

Cobra Pose

Tree Pose

Seated Forward Bend

Notes

_____

_____

_____

_____

_____

_____

_____

_____

_____

_____

_____

_____

_____

_____

Chapter Six

Use It or Lose It

"First we form our habits, then our habits form us."
– Author Unknown

The Importance of a Daily Practice

After the initial burst of enthusiasm, often we slack off on our practice, forgetting the many benefits obtained through the improvement of our health. But with this kind of work (inner journey), continuity and perseverance are required. We will progress more effectively through a daily practice. When we are not well, we turn to our practice. But perhaps illness could have been prevented or avoided if we had kept our bodies in full health. Having a daily practice means not to always have to be doing the physical asanas. Relaxation, rest, meditation, and even the simple art of walking can allow us the opportunity to be more present and aware of our thoughts and actions (more on these aspects of yoga in upcoming chapters).

The Advantages of Doing Yoga

- Frequent yoga practice clearly makes you physically stronger and more flexible.

- You will get taller as you eliminate the curve along the back of your spine.

- You will be able to stand for longer hours without getting tired, as you learn to "properly" stand on your feet.

- You are going to have better digestion and elimination.

- You will sleep better and need fewer hours, as your body will be more relaxed during the night.

- Health is wealth! And health is freedom. When you are healthy, you will be better prepared to combat illnesses.

- You will find balance in yoga. You are going to straighten yourself out if one part of the body is weaker than the other, by paying attention while doing your yoga poses. By continuing this awareness and attention throughout the day, you will reach a better balance, not just physically but a balance in life.

- Yoga is a way of looking at life; it changes who you are, and therefore changes the way you relate to others and respond to your environment.

How to Practice

Before we get started with our practice, there are some basic yoga principles I wish to review:

- Yoga is not competitive; be patient with yourself and do not concern yourself with others. Your body will "move" when it is ready. You must learn to listen to your body. Remember, you will improve over time, no matter what your starting level.

- Move slowly into and out of the postures, with full awareness of all the sensations flowing throughout

- Use yogic breathing during your routine. We move in and out of postures with the breath guiding us.

- Challenge yourself but don't strain. Be aware, and respect the healthy limit of your body's flexibility, and the place where your mind is naturally focused. It is at the point where your feelings of discomfort are heightened, that you have reached your limit. Going past this point brings pain, which is a clear signal from your nervous system that damage is occurring. Habitually going beyond your limitation, and causing yourself unnecessary pain, is often the result of a psychological need to prove something to yourself or someone else. If you force yourself into stretches beyond your body's limit to tolerate, your practice will create tension and stress instead of releasing it. And you may very likely injure yourself.

- "No Pain, No Gain" is not a moot that applies to yoga! Learning the difference between pain and discomfort is essential to a safe yoga practice. Movements that repeatedly cause pain should not be performed. You need to tell your instructor if you feel any pain. You may be advised to not do a particular thing at all, or a modification may be suggested. I tell my students that if using a scale from 1 to 10, with 1 being no pain and 10 being pain, we don't go past a 3 on the scale. The way I differentiate between discomfort and pain, is to ask yourself how you are feeling after a session. You may have feelings of having just "awakened" some muscles, and this discomfort goes away in a day or two. If, however, there is a real discomfort (pain) that lingers for the rest of the week, this would be an appropriate time to notify your instructor or health practitioner.

- Don't eat a large meal immediately prior to your practice. As you know, there is much twisting and turning, and you will feel uncomfortable on a full stomach. On the other hand, don't practice on an empty stomach; you may feel lightheaded. So just have something "light" to eat prior, like a piece of toast or fruit

- Taking time to "pause" in a posture is essential to gaining yoga's full benefits. As we and the postures are not created the same, how long we can hold a pose will differ. Some people will be able to hold a posture for only a few breaths, while others much longer. There is no need to have to endure the posture—just welcome the challenge while embracing what occurs when you relax and breathe while holding the pose. It is in the time between holding poses, and before releasing to pause, that we let go of any stresses or tension. I believe that in these "pauses," it is where transformation happens.

Creating Posture Sequences

In the early stages of a yoga practice, many people experience an initial burst of enthusiasm. Their time on the mat has left them feeling stronger, more flexible, calmer, and with a sense of progressing forward in their practice. This inspiration is difficult to sustain but learning how to create your own yoga sequence is an essential aspect of yoga. There is a logical underlying sequence, which is to flow naturally with the movements in your body. For example, easier stretches flow naturally into more difficult and challenging poses. After bending forward, a counter stretch (backbend) would help restore balance.

Energetically demanding postures are balanced with moments of rest. Gentle movements, and taking time to pause, assist in releasing tension. In my classes, the whole body is warmed up, powerfully stimulated through the poses, and cooled back down as the flow of postures comes to an end. Relaxation comes naturally at that time. The overall result is that you feel a profound sense of rejuvenation and balance.

The following are a certain series of postures done in proper sequencing that will allow you the opportunity to experience what works for you and what does not. After you become familiar with them, you can begin to personalize the routine to suit your needs. Be sure to listen to your body and give yourself permission to freely adapt the posture based on what feels right for you. If a certain posture causes you to strain, modify or substitute an easier form of the same stretch. For example, Tree pose is often difficult for people trying to balance on one leg. A modification would be to not completely lift your foot off the floor. Just lift the heel and lean it against your ankle. Or use a chair to hold onto as you balance.

You can expect gains in strength, flexibility, and focus. With these, there is a natural tendency that will draw you to "exploring" postures previously beyond your reach. This is a sign that your practice is evolving. Beyond a regular practice, a willingness to "play"—as I would encourage my students to do—is all that is needed to learn the finer points of yoga sequencing. Listen to your body for what feels right.

The posture sequences taught in most traditional yoga schools are suited to the physically proficient practitioners. Many of the yoga poses require core strength, and this should be addressed in specific preparatory exercises. Beginning students are often instructed to start practicing the traditional sequences by simply doing their best and omitting any postures that are too difficult. They are expected to develop, through repetition, the fitness and flexibility required to properly perform the routine.

Often, postures that stretch the spine intensely in one direction are followed by another set of stretches in the opposite direction, which is fine. But little time is given between postures for rest and compensatory movements that relieve any strain. Very few yoga students develop the ability to do "pretzel" postures. However, almost anyone can progress to a moderate practice that allows them to feel a better quality of health and well-being. In my classes, I refer to a good sequence as one that has "rhythm" to breathe in and breathe out. The postures are "layered" movements, from simple stretches to challenging postures, to "closing" (ending) poses.

Sample of a Posture Sequence

The following is a sample of how I may structure a class using poses that have been described in the previous chapters (review the "How to Do" section). I have included a few new counter stretches here but will explain. Let's get started—enjoy!! I believe that if you follow this sequence diligently, you can improve your flexibility, muscle tone, and concentration. Also, it is very likely you'll experience several other benefits as well, such as better sleep, better digestion, and stronger stamina. This is a simple routine; you just need to take the first step and get started. Remember the tips on how to practice. Most of the postures have been described in previous chapters, including the warm-ups and proper breathing.

- Begin with a short relaxation. (Refer back to Chapter three, in the section about warming up before stretching, and in the "How to Do" section.) This is a transition time, from your busy world to your yoga sanctuary practice. It is a time of "*letting go.*"

- Next is the warm-ups. I start out with simple warm-ups that take you through all the movements of the spine— forward/backward, up/down, side to side, and twist. Don't forget: to hold, but don't hold the breath, rest/pause, and release. There is an underlying logic to this sequence and an unfolding of exercises that makes sense to the body. I often begin warming up with spinal rock and rolls and "running the mat." But please refer to Chapter one on warming up, for all the possible warm-ups you could and should include. This part of the sequence prepares the muscles and joints and loosens the fascia to allow for maximum benefit of the postures, and to prevent injury.

• Now we begin to move from the warm-ups to the asanas. (And again, I refer to Chapter four, on the asanas, in the "How to Do" section.) From a seated position, move into a forward bend. While remaining seated on the floor, roll over to lie on your stomach. Come into Cobra posture. From Cobra, push yourself up into Table pose (on hands and knees with spine neutral). Cat and Dog stretch, while in Table pose, allows you to naturally flow into Downward Dog stretch.

• From Downward Dog pose, "walk" your feet toward your hands, and "roll up" one vertebra at a time, to standing. Once standing, twist side to side, allowing your arms to swing in front and behind, releasing out the lower back. Come to center and stand tall in *Tadasana*.

• From *Tadasana*, move into Triangle pose –repeat on both sides.

• Come back to *Tadasana* and move into Tree posture.

• Out of Tree posture, come back down to the floor and prepare for an inversion posture. (Refer to Chapter four for instructions.)

• The sequence ends with a longer relaxation in the posture *savasana,* which leads us to the next chapter. Read on for another "tool" that yoga has to offer for releasing stress and tension in the body.

Each yoga posture exists on a spectrum of difficulty. Recognizing this fact, you can structure your practice to move from the gentle to more challenging degrees within the same posture. The understanding of posture progression is that gentle poses prepare the body for more difficult postures. But what is most important is that there is a balance of postures that include all the movements of the spine.

There is a diagram at the end of this chapter depicting the principal of oppositional stretching. This is necessary to maintain proper alignment and flexibility. To keep your practice safe, and to get the greatest amount of benefit, you must first master the correct form in each posture. Thus, I recommend beginning yoga with a certified yoga instructor. It seems that once postures are mastered, your ability to create yoga sequences yourself will unfold naturally. And if mastering the willpower to practice regularly seems like too much for you, don't despair. One of the most amazing things about yoga is that it is both a discipline and a tool that *promotes discipline.* There is something about doing yoga every day that makes you *want* to do it every day!

Posture Sequence

You can observe in the below diagrams the principal of applying oppositional stretches to enhance the strength and flexibility of the spine, and balance in the body.

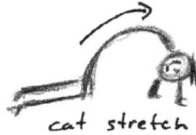

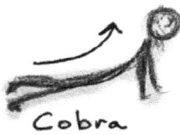

Table pose

cat stretch

dog stretch

Cobra

downward dog

mountain pose

triangle pose

tree pose

Shoulder stand

savasana

Notes

_____

_____

_____

_____

_____

_____

_____

_____

_____

_____

_____

_____

_____

Notes

Chapter Seven

Time to Relax

"Don't seek, don't search, don't ask. Don't knock, don't demand—relax! If you relax, it comes. If you relax, it is there. If you relax, you start vibrating with it."
– Osho

Living with your mind and body in harmony is our natural state. The key to good health, vitality, and peace of mind is *relaxation.* Yoga recognizes the mind-body connection, and the state of one influences the other. If your muscles are relaxed, then your mind must be relaxed. However, all action begins in the mind; if the mind is anxious, then the body is negatively influenced. When the mind receives a stimulus that alerts it to the need for action, the fight or flight response pattern kicks in. A message from the brain is sent via the nerves, to contract the muscles in readiness to respond. In this hectic world of ours, the mind is continually bombarded with stimuli that alert us to be on guard. The result is that people spend much of their lives, even while asleep, in a state of physical and mental tension. Physically, people hold tension often in their necks and backs. Mentally, holding tension through worry, depression, and fatigue is such a drain of our energy resources. The alternative to tension is *relaxation.*

The Relaxation Response

The counterpart to the flight or fight response is the *relaxation response.* The relaxation response appears when the body does not feel threatened, and the autonomic nervous system returns to normal. In other words, the relaxation response is the opposite of your body's stress response. During times of stress, the body's physiological state is alerted with an increase in heart rate and blood flow, and there is an increase in the release of hormones like adrenaline and cortisol, all preparing the body to fight or run. This response occurs naturally and, in ancient times, worked well for survival. This stress response was usually triggered by the need to avoid or challenge some predator. However, in these modern times, where we live in stress-provoking societies, the stress response is on constant alert, and the relaxation response does not have a chance to naturally follow before the next stressor is perceived. This chronic stress leads to the body being in a constant state of alert over perceived threats that are numerous and not always life threatening. This can lead to decreased immunity and other physical health issues, as well as negative mental health consequences like anxiety and depression.

Yoga can show you how the relaxation response can be cultivated through certain techniques that relax your body and mind. Yoga facilitates releasing bodily tension through many techniques, including breathing exercises and the postures, but especially through relaxation exercises. Meditation is also a great stress reliever because it works well for calming the mind and the body (more on meditation in the next chapter). In yoga, we physically relax the muscles by *letting go* of tension. Also, in yoga, one of the essential elements in yogic philosophy, and a moral discipline, is *non-attachment.* It is the fifth of the yamas mentioned in Chapter one. Non-attachment can be difficult to learn, especially in our present world where accumulating things is the norm. Attachment also means ownership. Many people who have progressed toward being less attached to worldly possessions have done so through yoga and meditation. Yoga helps you control your breath, your body, and your mind in a non-judgmental way. You become more accepting of yourself and more *RELAXED!* Practicing non-attachment can change the way you think about yourself, others, objects, and places. The more you practice non-attachment, the easier it is to live a physically and emotionally healthy life. And learning to let go may be one of the best things you ever do, and when you get it, you will feel free!

Benefits of "Letting Go" and Deep Relaxation

* Feeling of inner peace

* Enjoy being who you are

* Greater emotional stability

* Feeling more in control

* Many possible physical benefits, including lower blood pressure, fewer headaches, and better brain function

Relaxation is not so much a state of being but rather a progressive process with levels of increasing depths of relaxation. It is a matter of *letting go* versus holding on. As you relax your whole body, and breathe slowly and deeply, certain physiological changes occur. There is a decrease in activity of the nervous system. You consume less oxygen, and muscle tension is reduced. Even just a few minutes a day of deep relaxation will reduce fatigue and worry more effectively than many hours of restless sleep.

The Benefits of Deep Relaxation:

- The body can release not only surface tension, but sometimes deeply layered physical and emotional stress.

- The body and mind become revived, restored, and rejuvenated.

- It helps manage stress.

- It quiets the mind.

- Relaxation is a time to heal. I am reminded of the cartoon character, Daniel Tiger, who always says "rest is best" when you are sick.

Relaxation is not quite the same as doing nothing. It is a process that requires conscious effort to clear and *unblock* your body and mind. When you are truly relaxed, your body and mind and breath move together harmoniously in the body. Relaxation doesn't require any special devices, but the following may help you feel more comfortable, and make it easier to relax.

Tips for a Successful Relaxation Practice

- Practice in a quiet place, where you are not going to be disturbed. In my classes, I request students to turn off cell phones, etc. I do play soft music, which my students seem to enjoy, and they tell me that it helps them to relax.

- If lying down, to lengthen out the back of the neck and to support the chin moving down, place a small pillow under your head. If you feel discomfort in your lower back, place a large pillow or bolster under your knees for support.

- To ensure that your body stays warm, and to keep your energy within, cover yourself with a blanket. As the body relaxes, its surface temperature tends to drop, so an extra layer of clothing, like a sweater and socks, may be put on prior to entering relaxation.

- If you wear eyeglasses, take them off and place them on your chest. That way you know where they are, and I won't step on them. Some people like to cover their eyes with an eye pillow.

- It is not uncommon for people to fall asleep from time to time during a relaxation exercise. Eventually, and with practice, you will learn to relax completely while remaining aware of what is happening.

To truly relax, you must understand and practice the skill. Let's get started!!

Relaxation Techniques

There are many relaxation techniques used in present times, and all are valuable. In this section, I will present specific relaxation exercises and techniques that are an essential part of your yoga practice. You will be able to tap into these techniques whenever you need them. And relaxation may become one of your favorite yoga tools to combat stress and tension.

The Corpse Pose – *Savasana*

In yoga, the relaxation pose is known as *savasana*, and it is also widely known as the "Corpse" pose. This posture can be the simplest yet most difficult because you don't have to use any part of your body. Doing nothing is sometimes very difficult. The Corpse pose is an exercise in mind over matter. Just looking at the pose, outwardly looks like a corpse. But inwardly, the mind is fully awake and aware of all the sensations going on in the body. It is only with the help of the breath and the mind that it is easy to learn how to calm and relax the body, and to really look inward.

How to Do:

- Lie on your back with the legs extended, with feet hip-width apart. Bring the arms by your sides, palms up and fingers slightly curled (think of a baby's fingers).

- Close the eyes; draw your senses inward. Let the whole body relax and sink into the floor.

- Focus your attention on the flow of the breath, simply watching. Inhale naturally and, gradually over time, let the exhalation lengthen.

- Feel the heartbeat grow slow and steady.

- Release any conscious control of the breath.

- Scan all your body, from your heels to your head, to check that they are relaxed.

- Finally, let go into a deep relaxation, allowing all your worries and fears to fall away. Focus on how you are feeling in this deep state of relaxation. Try to bring this relaxed feeling with you as long as possible.

- When finished, open your eyes, and slide your arms along the floor and up over your head. Clasp your hands, bring your feet together, point the toes, and stretch. Hold and then release. This stretch is a full body stretch and a massage of the nervous system. My teacher, Nitya, introduced me to this stretch, and it can be done anytime throughout your practice.

It is best to allow the relaxation to end on its own. As you begin to listen to your body, it will naturally bring you out of the relaxation when it has adequately benefited. Try for 5 to 10 minutes to begin with; however, the longer the better. If you need a sound to remind you to return to waking consciousness, use an alarm clock that would not startle you. With practice, you will be able to set a "mental" clock, so that once closing your eyes, you will intuitively know when to end your relaxation.

Relaxation can be done in many ways. I will show you two ways: One is "dynamic," where you tense/release, usually done at the beginning of my classes; and the second way is a longer, guided relaxation to end the yoga class.

Tense/Release Relaxation Technique

This technique, I use at the beginning of my yoga session. I think of this as a transition time from our busy day outside to coming into the quiet, calm place of our practice. It is a time for the body and mind to *let go* of the busyness of all the activities in life. I ask my students to physically relax the body, and to mentally *let go* of all the worries, concerns, decisions, etc.

Benefits of Tense/Release Technique:

This relaxation technique asks you to physically tense (hold) different parts of the body, beginning with the limbs and eventually tensing the whole body, and then releasing (relaxing). This deeply relaxes the muscles and, almost immediately, you can feel release, and vitality awakened.

How to Do:

- Lie flat on your back in *savasana* (Corpse pose).

- With your eyes closed, focus your attention on your legs. Contract the muscles in your feet by pointing your toes straight ahead. Hold for a couple of seconds, tense, and then consciously release. Do the same with the muscles in your calves, upper legs, buttocks, and back.

- Bring your awareness to your arms, hands, and fingers. Make a fist and lift your arm slightly off the floor. Hold, tense, and then release!

- Draw shoulders up toward your ears. Hold, tense, and release!

- Make a "prune" face by squeezing your eyes, your mouth, and cheeks together. Hold, tense, and release!

- The tension should be done in a progressive manner, from mild tension to higher tension. *Deeply breathe* and *inhale* through your nose as you tense, and as you release, exhale, and let the breath be free. Scan all your muscles, from feet to face, to check that they are relaxed. You may wish to repeat this technique a few times. Each time focus on the increasing bodily sensation of no tension. At the end of your session, before opening your eyes, form the intention to keep this relaxed feeling as long as possible.

Guided Relaxation Technique

This technique is a longer exercise, usually done at the end of a class, after the warm-ups and the asanas. In my 60-minute class, I set aside 10 minutes at the end to consciously relax the body.

Benefits:

- This time allows you to "assimilate" all the benefits of yoga practice, with your body and mind. It helps you take inspiration of your session into the rest of your day.

- In this state of relaxation, the body and mind become refreshed, recharged, and rejuvenated.

- With regular practice, even just 5 minutes of relaxation will help combat the effects of chronic stress.

- The nervous system becomes quieter.

- Layers of tension, known and unknown, melt away.

- You learn to stay present and focused on what is going on in your body and mind.

How to Do:

This relaxation technique utilizes your power of imagination and auto-suggestion. If you can visualize things easily in your mind, you'll find this exercise fun and refreshing.

- Do this either lying down or sitting. Close your eyes, because when the outer eyes are closed, we are drawn inward, and our inner eyes begin to open.

- Still with eyes closed, begin to watch your breath as you breathe through your nose. Notice how it is cold as it flows in, and warm as you breathe out. Let the breath be quiet and shallow.

• Continue following the breath; feel the rise and fall in your chest. Inhale freely; exhale "forever" (long).

• Now bring your awareness down to your feet. Silently suggest: "My feet and ankles are relaxed." *Feel* them relaxed.

• Now slowly bring your awareness to your calves, thighs, and buttocks, continually suggesting relaxation to each muscle.

• Move your attention to your lower back, shoulders, arms, and hands. Feel the sensation of *release and warmth.*

• Focus on your face and eyes. Relax your mouth; have a slight gap between the upper jaw and lower. Relax the tongue.

• Now bring your awareness back to your breath and continue to relax into the stillness of the body and mind. If the mind wanders, which is normal, go back to focusing on your breath, watching it as you inhale and exhale.

Coming out of the relaxation consciously is important. Begin by moving just your pinky finger, then all fingers. Rotate your wrists and then your ankles. Bring your feet together and slide your arms overhead. Clasp your hands and stretch side to side. Take an enjoyable yawn and release your arms down; relax the whole body. If lying down, roll over to your right side, using your right arm as a pillow. When you are ready, push yourself up to a seated position.

After the relaxation, it is a good time to reflect on any insights that may have been discovered. For example, you may ask yourself what positive feelings or qualities were found that could strengthen, nurture, or improve your life (qualities of strength, flexibility, and renewed energy). How can you apply these insights and qualities to your life every day?

Making Time to Relax

Now that you are aware of all the benefits of relaxing and how to relax, it is a question of making it a priority to find the time to relax. We live in this stress provoking way of life, where the habit is to always do more and go faster. Unless, as individuals, we are willing to examine our priorities and change them, we are not likely to solve our problems with stress and stress-related illnesses. It is going to require discipline to schedule time for relaxation.

Taking a vacation is a very important way to cut stress—that is assuming you can afford to take a vacation. And if you go on a vacation, are you bringing along work—your cell phone and laptop?? I'd say, you really can't let go! I tell my students that making time for relaxation could be a simple "fit-in" through the day and is really substituting one habit for another. I remember being at work, at break time, walking around my office building. (Donna and I would often walk a couple of times a day.) Or instead of a coffee break, close the office door and do some deep relaxing breathing. At home, rather than watching TV, read or chat on the phone with a friend. (Yes, hear their voice.) If you could lie in *savasana,* once a day for 5–10 minutes, this deep relaxation can be a reminder that with all that is constantly going on around us, there is a quiet, peaceful place within that we can easily tap into.

The ability to relax the body, while the mind remains present and aware, is what makes deeper states of consciousness accessible. Besides all its health benefits, yoga teaches that learning to relax is a necessary step on the path of meditation. So, time to meditate! See the next chapter on how to meditate.

www.thebreatheandrelaxbook.com

Notes

_____

_____

_____

_____

_____

_____

_____

_____

_____

_____

_____

_____

_____

Chapter Eight

Time to Meditate

*"Embrace silence since meditation is the only way
to truly come to know your Source."*
— Wayne Dyer

The previous chapters have given you both an intellectual understanding and a physical experience of this discipline. You have been introduced to some technical principles involved, and you can breathe, align your body, and relax in ways that prepare you for the final phase of this journey called *yoga*. You don't need to formally meditate to practice yoga, although it is believed that the purpose of yoga is to prepare you for meditation. This chapter will deepen your understanding of what meditation is, inform you of the many benefits, and guide you in beginning a practice of your own.

What Meditation Is

If I were to describe meditation, I would say that it is a *way of training your mind to slow down, to be a "witness," one who can observe and not be reactive.* Meditation brings me to a place where I can stop the constant chatter that is going on in my mind. It is a workout for the mind. And like any workout, results are met only with practice and discipline. The best results occur with consistency over time. Just like any new exercise program, you just have to jump in and start. Start by trying for even a few minutes.

A few words about what meditation is not:

- It is not about stopping your thoughts or emptying your mind. It is a way to slow down and observe your thoughts without making judgment.

- Meditation is not a check-out of reality, like drinking excessive alcohol or using illegal drugs. Meditation is about checking in with yourself.

- It is not about absolute stillness of the body. Meditation can be experienced while walking, sitting, standing, or lying down.

Benefits of Meditating

The yogi masters have known for many years that the benefits of meditating are both psychological and physiological. After meditating for some time, you may feel different and notice changes in the following ways:

- Physical health can improve (lowered blood pressure, improved immune system).

- Helps combat chronic fatigue syndrome and more.

- Mental health can improve (better brain health; able to cope and manage stress better).

- Can help reduce anxiety and depression.

- Improvement in emotional health. With enhanced physical and mental health, you may experience an increase in positive emotions, and a decrease in negative thoughts.

- Can help with positive self-image.

- Enhances awareness; promotes our ability to recognize choices we have.

- Awakens willpower and strength.

- Teaches you how to skillfully manage your thinking. It can be a huge relief to know that not every thought needs to be developed.

Tips on Starting Your Own Meditation Practice

Before you begin to meditate, there are some steps you can take to prepare.

- Finding the right time – Choose a time that is convenient for you and your life. It's best to find a time that will work consistently for you. I highly recommend practicing every day. Some people add to the end of their asana practice or set aside another block of time. Traditionally, the morning is considered ideal because you are less likely to be distracted by the demands of your day. Many people find that a morning meditation helps them begin the day with a degree of equanimity and grace. However, if mornings are not convenient, try afternoon or early evening. The important thing is that you find a time that works best for you.

- Create a sacred space – To establish consistency, meditate at the same time and place every day. Choose a place that is quiet, a place where you will not be disturbed. It should be a space that inspires deep peace within you. It could be a corner in a room, or a walk-in closet. You may wish to have a meditation cushion or pillow, a blanket, and your yoga mat. People often set up a small alter with pictures or objects that are sacred to them. I have a small table with a candle and some flowers. Anything can be placed on your alter; anything that is uplifting and brings you to that place of joy, peace, and stillness within.

- Position – Traditionally, meditation is done sitting on the floor, but you may prefer a chair. The most important consideration is to be able to sit comfortably with a straight spine. You need to be free from distractions and pain.

- Length of time meditating – Don't try to do too much, too soon; you'll likely get discouraged and stop all together. In the beginning, start with a 3-minute or 5-minute meditation, and work up to 15 minutes. When first learning, don't go for length but go for depth. Meditation "clears" the brain, leaving you feeling fresh, clear, and calm; that is the feeling you want after your meditation practice.

Ways to Meditate

There are as many ways to meditate as there are people who ask, "How do I meditate?" I am going to give you some specific techniques to guide you into your own version of meditation. Your goal will be to find what doesn't work; and better yet, what works for you.

- Gazing – This is a very basic approach to meditating, and one that may be easier to practice if you are a beginner. Gazing or concentrating on a specific object or point of focus, with eyes either opened or closed, is the format. Candle gazing is a popular form of this method, and one I use in my classes. Focusing on a flower is another possibility. Traditionally, yoga masters would meditate on a particular deity.

- Breath – Using the breath as a point of focus is a good place to start as well. It is certainly convenient, and you count the breaths. Meditating on the breath means just observing it as it is, without changing it. The breath becomes the sole object of your meditation. You observe each sensation as it moves through the body—the nose, your abdomen and torso, etc. Observe how it feels as you inhale and exhale, noticing the temperature and the steadiness of the breath flow. Though you are fully aware of each detail, you are only observing, without comment or judgment. What you discover is neither good nor bad; you simply allow yourself to be with the breath, from movement to movement. The yoga masters believe that this breath observance is a direct channel to your true self.

- The Use of Sound – The word *mantra* is a Sanskrit word: *man* means "to think," and *tra* suggests "instrument." Thus, mantra is an instrument of thought. Traditionally, you would receive a mantra from a teacher, someone who knows you and your personality and needs. The act of repeating your mantra is called *Japa,* which means recitation. You would repeat your mantra as a way of meditating. Silently repeating the word *OM* is commonly used. Reciting a prayer or chanting is also used in meditating.

- Chanting – Chanting comes from the yogic tradition of believing that sound is a powerful force that is healing and sacred. Chanting invokes deeper concentration and devotion. It calms the mind and improves awareness. Many beginners find mantras relatively easy to do, but chanting intimidating initially. Personally, chanting in a group meditation, where the teacher leads the chant and the students repeat it, is a favorite of mine.

I have just given you a few ways to meditate. Meditation is simply the practice of bringing your body and mind into a deep state of calm. And most of us will admit that in our busy, often stressful lives, we could use some calm. I hope you will give meditation a try by experiencing the following guided, **seated** meditation.

Guided Seated Meditation

- Let's get started by getting into position for meditation. Sit comfortably on the floor or a chair. The most important thing is that your spine remains upright. If sitting on the floor, you may wish to place a cushion or folded blanket under your buttocks, to elevate the hips and gently allow your knees to fall toward the floor. You may also try putting folded blankets under your hips. Sit crossed leg. Relax your arms and place your hands on your thighs, palms up or down. Relax the shoulders; chin is level with the floor. Now that we are settled in, let's begin the meditation, using the breath to focus on.

- Try to bring yourself fully present. Begin to breathe deeply, using the three-part breath. Do this slowly so as to deeply relax the body, oxygenate the blood, and calm the nervous system.

- To begin the meditation, focus your attention on the natural flow of the breath. This can be done by bringing awareness to the nostrils; this is where the movement of air, in and out of the body, is easy to observe. Next, bring your awareness to your belly, and watch as it rises and falls. Apply no effort to control the breath. But pay attention to the rhythm of the breath flow. Notice if it is even or unsteady, deep or shallow.

113

Make no changes; just simply watch the breath naturally and spontaneously as it moves within you.

- As your concentration deepens, expand your awareness to the sensations being experienced in other parts of the body. Draw your attention to the area of strongest sensation. Stay there and observe your feelings and thoughts. Don't analyze, judge, or change. Just *let go* of the feelings and thoughts. Begin to recognize in your experience what is pleasant and worth keeping and push away what is painful. But again, let go of any need to change your experience in any way.

- If the mind starts to wander, simply come back to watching the breath to regain focus. It is common to have to repeat this many times in a single meditation.

At the end of every meditation, take time to just be. Release any effort to focus the mind. Sometimes ending a meditation with a prayer, or offering gratitude for your experience, is very satisfying.

How Do You Know If It Is Working?

- Meditation summons up feelings of mental calm and physical comfort, and the ability to be present in the moment-to-moment life experiences. As your meditation practice deepens, your ability to connect with your inner wisdom is enhanced, and you can stand back and take an optimistic view of life's situations.

- As you connect with yourself, your true core beliefs and values will appear and replace any inaccurate, outdated traits. Even painful life events can be viewed in an objective and calm manner.

- As meditation awakens awareness and asks that you not make judgment or changes but to step back and be a "witness," you can then be able to fully exercise the power of choice.

- As your clarity of judgment and willpower is increased, greater intuitive insight will also strengthen.

- You will become more balanced and stronger. So be patient! These are all indications of your progress, and that your meditation practice is working for you!

Yoga is not just a belief system or even just a practice; it becomes the *consciousness* in which we live. It is a way to express your authentic self through actions—the actions in your everyday life. The next chapter, the final one in this book journey, offers ways to be happy and reduce stress every day, all day!!

Notes

_____

_____

_____

_____

_____

_____

_____

_____

_____

_____

_____

_____

_____

Chapter Nine

Seven Ways to Be More Mindful and Happier Every Day!

"Meditate. Breathe consciously. Listen. Pay attention. Treasure every moment. Make the connection."
– Oprah Winfrey

In this book, we addressed both the intellectual understanding of yoga, and the physical experience of this discipline. You were introduced to the philosophical concepts and the technical principles. You were given the tools of yoga, needed in order to better meet the objective of releasing tension and reducing stress in your life. Proper breathing, correct alignment of your body, and relaxing and meditating are the tools yoga has, to assist you in making your journey in life more enjoyable (and manageable). Yoga offers you the opportunity to become present or *mindful* in your life. To be mindful, we must increase our awareness in the present moment. When we are forced by the ever increasing demands of our world, whether it is work, or family, etc., and are rushing to complete as much as possible in any given day, we are missing out on becoming a fully active participant in what we are doing, and are unable to appreciate the moment. By allowing ourselves some *breathing time* to be more *present and mindful,* we can tap into our *inner wisdom,* which can awaken us to our full potential to live healthier and happier, and to have more prosperous and satisfying lives. Attending yoga classes or sitting in a meditation pose are not the only ways to be more present and mindful in our daily activities. Let me show you some other ways to enjoy your life every day, all day!! Just before we get to some of the many ways in which we can find mindful moments in our lives, let's make the connection between yoga and mindfulness.

Yoga and Mindfulness – The Connection

Yoga and mindfulness are entwined disciplines that work together to help us promote optimal health and well-being. Both practices work to empower you. They aim to quiet the mind in order to cultivate a deeper connection to and understanding of self. Yoga and mindfulness teach you to tune into your breath, pay attention to bodily sensations, and accept reality as it is in that moment.

If you recall from an earlier chapter, the definition of yoga, as translated in Sanskrit, is "union." Yoga is a body of techniques that allows us to connect with ourselves—body, mind, and spirit. Yoga involves a series of asanas (physical postures) and pranayama (breathing practices) that encourage optimal health. Yoga also incorporates meditation and mindfulness. Also, as discovered in previous chapters, *awareness* is one of the "tools" found in yoga. Within the teachings of yoga, meditation and mindfulness create a link and cultivate an awareness of the fact that both your body and your mind impact important aspects of who you are and how you function in life. In yoga, it is believed that your physical body is a temple and represents the foundation from which your mind operates. It would be common sense that in order to keep your mind as healthy as possible, it is imperative to keep your body healthy.

According to the ancient yoga texts, yoga asanas and pranayama are necessary to prepare the body for meditation. The body is healthy when it is able to relax and is strong enough to hold still. It is then that there are fewer physical disturbances that might distract from the practice of meditation. I tell my students that one of the purposes of yoga is to prepare the body for meditation. Meditations are practices that can enhance your focus and awareness to help promote a clear, stable, and healthy state of mind. When we meditate, we cultivate mindfulness. With mindfulness, we become completely present in our lives, acting and reacting to the world around us, from a state of calm and peaceful acceptance and understanding.

What Is Mindful Yoga?

Mindfulness is, simply stated, just being aware of whatever is happening now. It is the awareness and non-judgmental acceptance of "what is." We become the witness—not judging the experience as good or bad—just observing. All mindfulness seeks is to just be with your own experience moment to moment. Whatever you feel, simply notice it and accept it. Don't try to change anything.

The difference between Mindful yoga and the wide variety of yoga practices out there, is that the focus is in the mind-body awareness, as opposed to alignment details and the exact physical posture. The point is to cultivate mindfulness, using the asanas as the vehicle in which to do so, as in the Hatha yoga classes I teach. Bringing mindful awareness to any physical activity reminds us to focus on whatever we are doing in that exact moment, thereby transforming the moment into a form of meditation. Yogi Amrit Desai used to term yoga as "meditation in motion."

When I taught meditation classes, I would schedule them right after a yoga practice class, before a formal meditation sitting. Thus, the intent was that the body was physically ready to meditate. Also characteristic of my yoga classes was the emphasis on observing rather than reacting while practicing the asanas. Emphasis was placed on the importance of observing your mind and feelings while in a yoga pose and tapping into your inner wisdom. Once I gave instructions to the students on how to get into the posture, I would remind them to cultivate mindfulness by asking them direct questions. An example of the dialogue would be as follows: Bring your awareness to your breath. Is it shallow or deep? Are the inhalations and exhalations steady? Are there any sensations in your body? Is your mind beginning to wander, or are you staying present, observing? I would ask my students to use their breath to bring themselves back to the present, and to be a "witness" only to what may be happening in that moment. This practice helps students to be aware of their thought patterns, to be curious when the mind wanders, and to notice any irritations or judgments. Students begin to notice patterns and can then start to take control and change if necessary.

The Benefits of Yoga and Mindfulness

- Improves physical health – can release stress; improves quality of sleep

- Improves mental health – boosts positivity; helps alleviate negative emotions like anxiety and depression

- Improves overall well-being – gives insight into your feelings, and clarity in decision making; improves creativity

- Helps you face the challenges of everyday life – encourages you to be patient and not to readily react to situations

- Helps you to be more accepting – teaches you how to let go and accept situations for what they are in that moment

- Brings self-awareness to the body-mind connection developed through the practice of yoga – becomes a tool for transformation outside of your practice

- Teaches you to have more gratitude and spontaneity in life

Attending yoga classes or sitting in a meditation pose are not the only ways to be more present and mindful in our daily activities. Let me show you how else you can enjoy your life every day, all day long!!

How to Find Moments to Be Mindful Throughout Your Day

Try the following ways to be more mindful and present, from the moment you wake up to when you climb into bed. You may find you are more relaxed, less stressed, and worry-free. You are able to concentrate and better able to focus your energy on what is really important. And you will have a new appreciation of what is in your day and your life.

- When you wake up – Don't immediately jump out of bed when the alarm goes off. Take a moment to lie there; open *your* eyes and give them time to adjust to the light. *Listen* to the sounds around you. Then bring your *awareness* to your *breath*. Slowly begin to deepen your breath, bringing awareness to the sensation of your inhalations and exhalations. On each inhalation, notice the belly expanding as your lungs inflate and your chest rises. On each exhalation, notice the relaxing of your diaphragm as your belly softens and your lungs deflate. After a few rounds of breathing, *stretch*. Do a full body stretch and remember that this stretches the whole body and is a massage on the nervous system.

- As your coffee brews – Whether you're pouring your morning cup or waiting for the kettle to boil for tea, take to reading something inspirational and/or spiritual, or time to journal for a few moments. This may also be a good time to visualize what you would like your day to be like. To help set the tone for the day, I use this time to think of all I am grateful for in this very moment.

- At work – The key, while at the office, is to avoid multi-tasking, especially if you use a computer at work. I offer some suggestions: Set designated times to check your emails, and please, please do not "reply to all" if not necessary. Have only one browser open at a time. Also, to help remind you that a break is on order, use a prompt, such as when you hear the coffee brewing. Try to have a break at the same time every day and eat your meals away from your desk. You need to have a scheduled *"break time,"* because it is just that. Do some *deep breathing* or go for a *walk.* These scheduled times tell our minds to *focus* on a particular task, and only that task at the time. As you work, note any emotions and/or physical sensations that arise throughout the day. You may wish to record them. But just *observe* and be *aware.* The ability to recognize your emotions will allow you to be aware of your feelings as they arise. Being aware of what triggers certain emotions will help you choose your response in advance, rather than reacting after the fact.

- During your exercise time – Whether it is running, CrossFit, or yoga, etc., throughout your workout, be *aware* of your body, and notice changes in physical sensations. Start with the breath, then the muscles, and then your emotions. Pay *attention* to each movement; curiously explore the depth with which you go into it. I suggest to my students to "play" a little in the postures, testing the ways and limits in which their bodies are able to move. Remember to be *patient,* and to *accept* where you are at. The body will move when it is ready. Sometimes listening to music that you enjoy may help you better focus in your workout. I use soothing music in my classes. It becomes an auditory cue for the mind and body to relax.

- While preparing dinner – This is a wonderful time to get everybody involved. It is a perfect time to engage many senses; to smell, touch, taste, and visually take in each ingredient of your meal. By washing and chopping, and noticing the textures and colors, you use each sense; you can hear the sizzling as you sauté your meal. Try to use fresh, organic ingredients if you can. Remember: "Health is wealth," and as the Bible says, food is our medicine. You can mindfully place your food on your plate, making it pleasing to you by paying attention to detail and taking care. Food made with love, always tastes better.

- As you eat dinner – Before we eat dinner, my daughters and I take a moment to give a *blessing* over our food, to acknowledge how fortunate and grateful we are for the meal. Observe the food that has been thoughtfully prepared. Sit tall, be aware of your posture, and have your feet supported by the ground. Chew *slowly*. Take small bites; let the food mix with your saliva. It is the beginning of digestion. Take note of how the foods you are eating affect your emotions and thoughts. And *listen* to your body, bringing *awareness* to any physical sensations, especially those that indicate that you are full; and stop eating at that time.

- Getting ready for bed – This is the time when we want to conjure up the relaxation response, before we fall asleep. Certain prompts can help set the stage for a good night's sleep; for example, running a warm bath or playing soft music. When you are ready, get into your bed and sit upright comfortably. Close your eyes. And just as we started out our morning, begin to *focus* on your *breath,* noting the sensations and sounds of each inhalation and exhalation. As you focus on the breath, with each exhalation, *let go* of any physical tension, and *let go* of any mental busyness of the day. As thoughts arise, *acknowledge* and then disregard them, continuing to *come back to the breath. Do this* for a few minutes before you lie down, and then drift off to sleep.

The practices of yoga, meditation, and mindfulness have all been shown to help enhance physical and mental well-being, as well as to reduce stress. Through the practice of yoga, you can strengthen your body; through the practice of meditation, you can strengthen your mind, and together they will promote a more mindful state of awareness. Being mindful is not about changing who you are. It is about understanding that your thoughts don't have to control how you feel or act! Together, these practices will empower you to live your life to the fullest!

We need to slow down, breathe, and relax to be more mindful, and have the power to live effectively with less stress and more joy. The nature of our thoughts determines our pace in life. When the mind goes rushing from one frenzied thought to another, this over stimulation is toxic. One way to give time and planned effort in keeping your mind healthy is to lay the foundation right from the start of your day. I have developed a process that has assisted me in sorting and clarifying my thoughts and feelings. This has ultimately helped to get my day moving forward in a positive, productive way. Try this THREE MINUTE MORNING SPIRITUAL 'JAVA' to awaken your inner strengths. Meet the world with your highest self. This morning ritual has been most effective in my life. The difference in how I focus my day has been immediate and extraordinary. Go to my web page and discover this easy, convenient and enjoyable practice to give you your best possible day!

Notes

_____

_____

_____

_____

_____

_____

_____

_____

_____

_____

_____

_____

_____

Epilogue

*"There is something quite gratifying in taking charge
of your life. Either you can seize your own destiny,
or it will be thrust upon you."*
– Loreena McKennitt

You have finished the book. You have discovered that yoga offers practical and workable tools for stressing less and living with optimal health and fulfillment. Your ultimate goal in life is to become your best self. Your immediate goal is to get on the path that will lead you there. Yoga will show you the way! By being aware of ourselves through a detached, moment-to-moment watchfulness, we are able to see the direction we should follow to improve ourselves and live with less stress and more joy. Our energy should flow, unobstructed through us. Each of us has the power within to show ourselves our potential, and to guide us to our best selves.

Awareness is found in the body through the yoga postures. You can see physically what you are doing and where you are going. Awareness is energy. When we become aware, we simultaneously liberate our attention from the distracting emotion or activity and become free to choose another path. Eventually, as we awaken to our awareness, we can choose to turn our energies in more positive, self-supporting directions.

We become free to choose because of awareness; and the subsequent energy that is freed by our non-resistant, non-critical observing activities, is freeing. If we wish to control and manage the challenges in life, an excellent way to do so is to observe it objectively and without judgment when it shows up in our day-to-day choices. I must emphasize the importance of non-judgmental observation, or as referred to in this book, as being a "witness" only. When we can detachedly observe our emotions and thoughts, we can eventually control them.

Relaxation and meditation bring us inward, where we experience only each moment. There is no going forward or backward, but we are just present in the moment. This is *mindfulness*; it is objective awareness of ourselves as seen through our thoughts and actions. Anyone can, with practice and sincere intentions, become an objective observer of themselves. People can teach themselves about themselves, objectively, as they go about their daily routines. Routines often will bring to the surface valuable information about a person. Self-knowledge can be a cure to build up self-confidence in your own power to be happy in life. The life of inner peace, being harmonious and without stress, is the existence that can be found in our true selves.

Yoga tells us that there must be harmony between the body, mind, and spirit to lead us to know our true authentic selves—*self* being the unique totality of body, mind, and spirit in each of us. Each of us possesses the talents, wisdom, and creative powers to be successful and happy in life. Yoga can help! Each chapter of this book offers the tools of yoga: the poses, breathing exercises, relaxation, meditation, and mindfulness. Through the tools of yoga, insights and inner wisdom is found in awareness, observing, slowing down, being non-judgmental, acceptance, being present, etc. The tools of yoga lend themselves to the development and revelation of these qualities that underlie each layer of ourselves. Just as a fertilizer nourishes and promotes growth within a tree, the insights act as a catalyst for growth and discovery of your true authentic self, to live your best life. The Yoga 360° Intervention model, as shown in Chapter one, reflects the layers of self. I have included an additional model diagram at the end of this epilogue, reflecting some of the insights that can be derived through a yoga practice. The model is a visual aid to assist in contemplation of where you are and what you would need, to feel you are moving in the right direction to find balance in your life.

The diagram offers you an opportunity to ask yourself if an intervention in any area would be helpful in response to your current environment, at any given point in your life, as you are in a constant state of balancing and re-balancing where you are in your journey.

You can see the model diagram of the Yoga 360° at the end of this chapter. It should be in color, but it is not. It should be full size, but it is not. But at least you can get a hint of what I am talking about by gazing at this page. However, if you want to see the real model, just go to the website and get your copy there— download the full-size, full-color, print-ready model!

For me, yoga has been a journey of discovery into the many layers of self—body, mind, and spirit. I know it is the balance within these three layers that brings me happiness. Yoga has been a profound vehicle for helping me to not only cope with my daily stresses, but to answer the question, "Who am I?" I'm learning that part of getting to know oneself is being able to look at your life as both an inner and outer journey. It is not necessarily what I am doing or where I am going. I am not *doing*, but I am breathing and being mindful. We do not have to be all, or have all, to choose to act on behalf of what we value. The joy in this journey of life is not dependent upon reaching some goal or attaining the mountain peak. The joy comes from what transpires along the way. As I'm getting older, my physical, emotional, and spiritual needs have changed, and in many ways, yoga has helped me through those changes and challenges.

I am here to develop and grow, to do my share to make the world a better place, to make the world that is me, my inner world, as honest and as true to my authentic self as I possibly can.

This is a new day, a new choice. A new journey begins with your next right choice. Right choices resonate within us. Choosing rightly means that with each conscious choice, we choose to be our best selves—our most ethical and most generous selves—and we become more fully human. By choosing rightly and in the direction of what we truly want, and in accordance with our values, we learn about our strengths. We also notice our weaknesses. But we grow in insights and understanding. We can choose what is most helpful, and we feel our creative powers growing, which allows us to seize the opportunity of taking charge of our lives.

Every time we consciously choose something in line with what we feel is highest and best in ourselves, we support our true selves. Also, we reinforce the idea that we are good, valuable, and able to meet the challenges of life. This reinforces our next healthful choices. Thus, a more positive cycle takes hold of our habits, patterns of thinking, and outcomes.

We grow by moving step by step, choice by choice, in the direction of whatever it is our inner selves tell us that we need in any given situation to live our best lives. We must affirm our true selves through our choices. In this way, all choices and all day-to-day decisions have the energy to transform our lives if we are open to the messages and cues from our inner creative powers, and the way in which this power relates to our outer lives, in our relationships, our work, our decision making, how we spend our time, etc.

Right here, right now, we can act! Make the choice to begin a yoga practice. And with each practice time, we gain some measure of increased self-awareness, self-confidence, and self-esteem, and some measure of control over our lives. It is time to stress less, and SLOW DOWN AND BREATHE!

Take care of the house you live in (body, mind, and spirit) as you would the physical place in which you live. It is your temple. It takes conscious discipline and a concerted effort to maintain a healthy body and mind. Have patience and acceptance with yourself. It takes purposeful concentration and devotion of a daily practice to quiet the "chatter" of the mind. We must think less and feel more to be able to SLOW DOWN and JUST BREATHE! We must give preference to the positive lessons in our life experiences and be grateful for the "teaching" lessons. We must nourish hope and learn to trust and believe in ourselves. We can't drive a car forward while constantly looking in the rear-view mirror. A new journey begins with your next right choice.

We intuitively know what is "right" for us. We know ourselves better than anyone else. We are individually unique among seven billion people. Our inner wisdom makes us all "glorious" beings deserving of living our best lives!

While our physical paths may not yet have crossed, we now share a connection. It is clear now that we connect on a similar energetic, vibrational frequency. From my core essence, I wish you much joy in your spiritual journey. I believe that the highest form of love a person can have for another is to wish for them to evolve into the best person they can be—I wish this for you!! I hope our paths stay connected!

P.S.
If you're looking for more ways to bring an abundance of joy into your life and the lives of others, or if any of this material presented resonates with you, you may enjoy staying in touch by visiting my web page at thebreatheandrelaxbook.com.

Yoga 360° Intervention Model

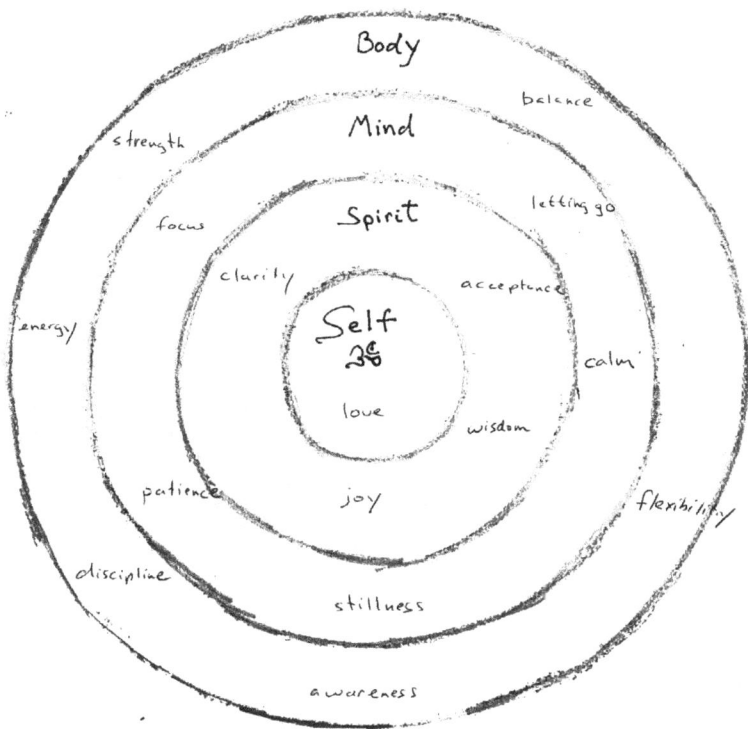

The model reveals to the eye all the strengths, talents, and creative powers that have always existed in our conscious.

As you will discover through your own yoga practice, there are endless insights to be found that will guide you along the path to your best life and best self. You may wish to add them onto this model. If you would like a full-page, colour, print-ready copy then please go to: www.thebreatheandrelaxbook.com.

Notes

About the Author

Amanda has resided, for most of her adult life, in Toronto, Canada, with her two extraordinary daughters, two dogs, two cats, and three fish. In the mid-80s, she began a career as a probation officer. At this same time, Amanda started practicing yoga. Yoga was her "sanity" as she witnessed others in her profession struggle with the stresses and pressures of the job. Yoga revolutionized her life, and this is one of the reasons Amanda wanted to write this book.

As a dedicated yoga practitioner, she has traveled to India, the United States, and throughout Canada, observing, studying with, and interviewing some of the world's leading yoga teachers. Amanda is very much qualified to reconcile ancient yoga teaching with modern day practice. Her travels and experiences led her to becoming a certified yoga instructor and a certified reflexologist. She also has numerous accreditations in the following areas: children's yoga, Kids Have Stress programs, Hallelujah Acres Health Minister, as well as training in dance kinetics, wellness in the workplace, and working with differently-abled persons and seniors' fitness.

Amanda commenced teaching yoga in various adult recreational and educational facilities. After a few years, she began teaching privately, hiring church halls for her classes. This allowed her to teach smaller groups. As her children grew, Amanda was inspired to learn the various values of yoga at the different stages of life. She is known for innovative play techniques while conducting children's and family circus classes and workshops. Her precision and dynamic energy were key to making yoga fun and safe! Over the years, she has expanded her teaching to include seniors; and at the present time, she is volunteering teaching for the Canadian Institute for the Blind.

For more than 30 years, Amanda has been transforming bodies and lives with her innovative holistic approach to health and happiness through yoga. Her teachings and observations incorporate the natural principals of the body and of the breath. Her self-styled techniques of achieving well-being is to listen to the body and mind, and work with them instead of against them to accomplish dramatic positive results.

Amanda's book explores her passion for yoga, and argues that yoga can have a profound effect on overall health and personal development. Amanda's most recent endeavor is teaching those in leadership roles to coach others on how to demonstrate and support all the benefits yoga has to offer. She is particularly interested in hearing from those persons providing a mentoring relationship role in their organization or in the community. She is available as a guest speaker or presenter, and can offer workshops. Amanda can be contacted via her website at www.thebreatheandrelaxbook.com.

www.ingramcontent.com/pod-product-compliance
Lightning Source LLC
Chambersburg PA
CBHW051843090426
42736CB00011B/1932